Praise for *Life Is* _____

"Judah is the most compassionate and giving person I have ever met. His teachings are easy to understand and full of truth and real life. I like Judah even though he dresses funny!!"

—BUBBA WATSON,
TWO-TIME MASTERS CHAMPION

"In a day and age of terror, fear, confusion, and chaos, so many people are wondering what exactly 'life is.' Judah Smith, in his engaging, relevant, fun, loving, and deeply profound way, helps us all to see exactly what this thing called life is all about. This is the book that you want to give to all your friends. Trust me."

—CHRISTINE CAINE,
FOUNDER OF THE A21 CAMPAIGN

"Life IS . . . so many things! Perhaps we can all agree, it is an adventure. Highs and lows, tragedy and triumph, crazy storms and smooth sunsets. And when it comes to navigating this journey called life, Judah Smith does it better than anybody I know. I've seen him preach his voice empty on the biggest of stages, in public. I've seen him cry his eyes empty mourning the loss of his beloved father, in private. I've seen him show love and compassion to the 'famous' and the 'faceless.' I've seen him lead his powerful church in the thousands, and lead his family of five, with even more grace. The only 'constant' in Judah's life is Jesus and His gospel. Perhaps there is something to that. This book is a must read."

—CARL LENTZ, CO-PASTOR,
HILLSONG CHURCH, NEW YORK CITY

"Judah's way of translating to everyone is incredible. He has no other motive but to help people. The best guy I know. Love you Judah."

—Justin Bieber,
singer-songwriter

"Judah has impacted my life deeply through his way of pouring God's Word into my everyday life. He has a voice, a way of communicating in such a relevant way, speaking truth into our generation. I'm grateful for his constant reminders of how much God loves me and the power of using my voice. He is, in my definition, a true leader."

—Selena Gomez,
actress and singer

"There are very few people in life that you can turn to for anything. Sometimes it is just a text, phone call, or a good hang. Other times it is some much needed advice or guidance. Whatever it is, I am lucky to say that Judah is one of those people for me."

—Rickie Fowler,
professional golfer

"Judah Smith is one of the most gifted communicators to grace this generation and I am honored that he would call me his pastor. His teaching style is as unique as his personal style; and you cannot leave his presence without feeling loved, valued, enlightened, and enlarged. His revelations based deep in biblical truth and his knowledge of the Word of God will deepen your spiritual understanding and open your eyes to what life—and the One who created it—is all about."

—Brian Houston,
senior pastor, Hillsong Church

"All we long for and everything we'll ever need are wrapped up in the stunning love of Jesus that pursues and perfects us. Judah Smith champions the heart of the Father's love once again with his fresh and unique voice in his latest, *Life Is _____*. Read it. Breathe it in. Believe it. Walk in it!"

—LOUIE GIGLIO, PASTOR,
PASSION CITY CHURCH AND
PASSION CONFERENCES

"If we're not careful, we can float through life without truly taking advantage of it. Are you satisfied, do you feel complete, do you know what God truly wants for you? Judah once again reminded me of these things in a powerful follow-up to *Jesus Is _____*."

—JASON KENNEDY, E! NEWS HOST

"Judah has an unbelievable ability to convey how God really feels about us as people. In a landscape littered with religious ideals and structure, Judah cuts through the rigors and delivers the simple message and truth that God undeniably and illogically loves us. Always has and always will."

—RYAN GOOD, PRODUCER OF
JUSTIN BIEBER'S BELIEVE; *JUSTIN
BIEBER: NEVER SAY NEVER*; AND
PUNK'D

LIFE IS _____.

LIFE IS_____.

GOD'S ILLOGICAL LOVE WILL CHANGE YOUR EXISTENCE

JUDAH
SMITH

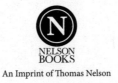

NELSON
BOOKS

An Imprint of Thomas Nelson

Published in Nashville, Tennessee, by Nelson Books, an imprint of Thomas Nelson. Nelson Books and Thomas Nelson are registered trademarks of HarperCollins Christian Publishing, Inc.

Published in association with the literary agency of Fedd & Company, Inc., P.O. Box 341973, Austin, TX 78734.

Thomas Nelson titles may be purchased in bulk for educational, business, fundraising, or sales promotional use. For information, please e-mail SpecialMarkets@ ThomasNelson.com.

Unless otherwise noted, Scripture quotations are taken from THE NEW KING JAMES VERSION. © 1982 by Thomas Nelson, Inc. Used by permission. All rights reserved.

Scripture quotations marked NLT are from *Holy Bible*, New Living Translation. © 1996. Used by permission of Tyndale House Publishers, Inc., Wheaton, Illinois 60189. All rights reserved.

Scripture quotations marked MSG are from *The Message* by Eugene H. Peterson. © 1993, 1994, 1995, 1996, 2000. Used by permission of NavPress Publishing Group. All rights reserved.

Scripture quotations marked NIV are taken from the Holy Bible, New International Version®, NIV®. Copyright © 1973, 1978, 1984, 2011 by Biblica, Inc.™ Used by permission of Zondervan. All rights reserved worldwide. www.zondervan.com

Library of Congress Cataloging-in-Publication Data

Smith, Judah.
Life is -- : God's illogical love will change your existence / Judah Smith.
  pages cm
Includes bibliographical references.
ISBN 978-1-4002-0477-9 (alk. paper)
1. Christian life. 2. Life--Religious aspects--Christianity. 3. Christianity--Philosophy. 4. Love--Religious aspects--Christianity. I. Title.
BV4509.5.S628 2015
248.4--dc23
                2014023618

Printed in the United States of America

15 16 17 18 19 RRD 6 5 4 3 2 1

To the love of my life, Chelsea Rene Smith

Contents

CONTENTS

Foreword

Russell Wilson

It is a true honor and with great excitement that I get the gracious opportunity to introduce my friend in Christ, Judah Smith. Judah is one of the most influential and inspiring people you come across in life due to his intense passion for life and people all over the world. He leaves you always wanting more and ultimately makes you a better person. His intense passion for the Word of God and willingness to dive deep into God's lessons creates a desire to learn more about Jesus. Although he is an amazing friend, amazing pastor, amazing Seattleite, an above average basketball player, and an excellent golfer (he thinks he is a mix of Larry Bird and Bubba Watson), he is most impressive when teaching who Jesus really is to *all* of us.

We are all friends of God. After ten minutes with Judah you discover his love for Christ, his love for his beautiful wife and family, Christians and non-Christians, and his church: City Church. Judah Smith has one mission in life: to express the importance of the desperate need we all have for Jesus to enter our lives and turn us inside out and make us completely brand-new.

One of my fondest moments of Judah Smith is when he talked to our team before we won Super Bowl XLVIII (48 for those of you who don't know your Roman numerals or simply weren't rooting for the Seattle Seahawks). Judah spoke from one of the most important scriptures of the entire Bible: 2 Corinthians 5:17, which reads, "Therefore, if anyone is in Christ, the new creation has come: The old has gone, the new is here!" (NIV).

This scripture is so imperative in growing in our relationship (yes, *relationship*!) with Jesus because we *all* fall short of the glory of God, yet through our mistakes in life and wrong decisions and sinful nature, Jesus is there to make us brand-new! We as Christians, as well as non-Christians, miss out on the simple fact that God sent his one and only Son, Jesus Christ, to die for our sins because of his miraculous love for us! As a result, we are cleansed and start each morning and day brand-new in hopes for our hearts to be solely focused on living for the one who died on the cross for our sins.

Judah explains Jesus' miraculous power, forgiving nature, and love for us not only in this amazing book you are about to read, but also in his constant quest to share his love for Jesus Christ to others.

Judah, I love you . . . in the most masculine friend way

possible. I am grateful for the man you have helped me become over the past couple of years and for all the encouragement every morning and every night as a brother in Christ.

I am FOREVER GRATEFUL for you, champ. #WeMadeIt

Love,

Russell Wilson

Friend of God &

Super Bowl XLVIII Champ

p.s. You won't want to put this book down . . .

Introduction

I recently had a conversation with a really smart person. I don't mean street-smart—I mean a bona fide, card-carrying member of the genius club. This individual spoke English, but it wasn't the English the rest of us speak.

We were talking about the Bible. Since I'm a pastor, I try to have a bit of a grasp on the Bible. But I wasn't tracking with the conversation at all. He was referencing all kinds of terms and topics and people, but I was totally lost.

Even his metaphors were too sophisticated for me. He was like, "For example, consider the metaphysical ramifications of the mushroom in medieval Mediterranean monasticism..."

And I was like, "Um, could you give me an example to explain that example?"

I started to think, *This might be a different Bible. This might even be a different language. I'm not familiar with any of the English this guy is currently utilizing.*

So like any humble, honest, secure person, I bluffed. "Oh, yeah. Completely agree. My thoughts exactly."

We weren't connecting. There was no relationship. Why? Because he was way beyond me. Intellectually, he wasn't just on another level, he was in another universe. There was a massive chasm between us, and it was going to take a heck of a lot of work for me—basically my entire lifetime—to dissect that thirty-second conversation.

I think sometimes we have a similar mentality toward God. He is so perfect, so great, so far removed, that we wonder if we can relate to him at all.

And even if we tried to relate to him, would he care about what we are going through right now? After all, he's running the entire universe. Does the fact that I lost my job or my temper or my keys matter to him?

It's easy to think the answer to questions like that is no. But the point of the Bible is that God is not too distant or disinterested to relate to us. On the contrary: God is with us, loves us, and wants us to be fulfilled and satisfied. God wants our lives to be awesome in every way.

That leads me to the premise of this book—that Jesus shows us how to live life to the fullest.

Life Is _____.

What is life? What are we here for? What is truly important? What will bring authentic satisfaction and lasting happiness?

We all ask these questions, and we all come to our own conclusions.

Personally, I think the most reliable source of answers is Jesus. Ethically, morally, socially, and emotionally, Jesus is a perfect example of a life well lived.

I don't know where you might be on the spectrum of belief in Jesus, and honestly, I'm not here to tell you where you should be. You might not be sure Jesus is God. You might not be sure he can forgive sins or needs to forgive sins. But we can learn a lot from Jesus, so let's start there.

Jesus had a lot to say about the nature and meaning of life. This book is built around four broad statements that I believe encapsulate his message:

1. Life is to be loved and to love.
2. Life is to trust God in every moment.
3. Life is to be at peace with God and yourself.
4. Life is to enjoy God.

If you have heard me speak or read my previous book, *Jesus Is*____, you'll know that I am not a particularly concrete sequential person. Consider this fair warning.

I'm not going to approach these four principles in a comprehensive, exhaustive way. Instead, I'm going to highlight some biblical stories and principles that have been helpful to me in my own walk with God and, I think, will be helpful to you.

It will be fun. It will be practical. And it will be a little random.

Just like life.

When I preach and write, I try to retell biblical stories in modern language. It's not a new translation; it's a paraphrase. It is my attempt to put myself in the shoes—well, sandals—of the original audience.

Maybe you aren't sure what you believe about the Bible, and I'm fine with that. But we can all learn from it. It was written to help real people facing real issues. It has stood the test of time, and its teachings have shaped cultures, governments, and nations.

When I read about Jesus' passionate love for people and his commitment to his purpose and cause, I am inspired to live the kind of life he lived. He is the perfect example of how to live life—with all its adventures, surprises, and delights—to the fullest.

LIFE IS <u>to be loved and to love.</u>

Life is to be loved and to love. The order of those two phrases is intentional, because until we realize we are loved, it's tough—probably impossible—to truly love.

Most of us have the privilege of being loved by at least one or two people on this planet, and hopefully by a lot more than that. However, the love that matters the most, the love that enables us to know we are valuable and significant, is God's love for us.

The more I think about God's love, the more I realize I will never fully understand it. This isn't one of those topics where you can cross every *t* and dot every *i*. God is outside our scope and our frame of reference, and his love is more than we can comprehend.

I'm going to try to describe it anyway, though, because you need to know that God loves you. I am convinced that's the main message of the entire Bible. *God loves you.*

Once we begin to grasp his love, it's a lot easier to love other people. There is something about God's love that helps us look past ourselves and see those around us.

Life is meant to be lived in love.

Love Chases

Chasing Spot

Awhile back I was shopping, which is one of my God-given gifts, and I walked by a spa. Now I'm not going to lie to you—I like spas. Sometimes my wife, Chelsea, and I will go to a spa and just hang out; maybe we'll even get a chair massage together. Spas are one of my happy places.

I had never seen this spa before. It looked beautiful. It had bright colors, and it was attractive, and I thought, *This is a really cool spa.* I was inches from walking in to check it out when, to my utter shock and horror, I realized that the reason the chairs were so small and the beds were so little was that this was a spa for animals. It was a spa where you paid real, human money so your *animals* could be massaged. And by the way, the prices were exactly the same as they are for a human massage.

I'm pretty sure that if you do get your pets massaged, they

are like, *What is going on? This is weird. Why are they doing this to me?*

I found that a little bit alarming, but I wrote it off. Maybe it was an anomaly. But then recently we were checking into a hotel, and they asked us, "Do you have any pets?"

And I thought, *Well, yes, I have a three-year-old and a five-year-old and an eight-year-old . . . Oh, they mean animals. My bad.* "No, we don't have any pets. We don't do animals."

Now, you should know that I come from a long line of animal lovers. During the first sixteen years of my dad's life, his family owned twenty-four dogs in total. No exaggeration. At one point they had nine at once. So I come from a line of animal lovers, at least on my dad's side. Now my mom—not so much.

I admit I do like dogs, at least from a distance and as long as they don't touch me. I definitely don't like cats. I don't really think anybody likes cats. I'm not sure if dogs go to heaven, but I know for sure where cats go.

So the lady at the hotel asked, "Do you have any pets?"

We said, "No."

She said, "That's too bad."

I said, "I don't mind it actually."

"It's just that the experience here for your pets is almost equal to your own experience."

"Come again? I'm a human being. You know, with a soul."

"Well, we have special clothing for your pets. We have a special bed for your pets. We have special outings for your pets . . ." And she kept going.

I thought, *This is really getting crazy. These are animals.*

These are four-legged creatures. These are domesticated beasts that drool and shed. And people are taking them way too seriously.

And it gets crazier. I was driving down a Seattle freeway, a freeway intended for humans, when suddenly cars started slamming on their brakes and skidding to a stop. And I thought, *Oh no! There's been an accident just ahead. It must be a bad one.* I even started praying, because human lives were at stake here.

Eventually we got to the front of the chaos, and there was a car stopped in the carpool lane. And I was thinking, *What is going on?* And then we saw a little cocker spaniel running his heart out down the carpool lane. And a human being, evidently little Spot's owner, was out of his car and was running down the carpool lane behind his dog.

That's right. A dog and his human were cavorting down a freeway meant for people and their vehicles. All the vehicles were skidding and sliding to a stop lest little Spot meet a tragic end.

It gets worse. Other humans started joining the search and rescue. They got out of their cars and started running down the freeway after Spot. It was madness.

Now I'm going to tell you why Spot was running away. It was because he didn't want any more massages, he didn't want any more outings, he didn't want any more clothes. Spot is an animal, and Spot wanted to be free!

But his owner was running down the freeway like a madman, and I was thinking, *This makes no sense. This is ridiculous. Humans are going to die for Spot.* It's irrational.

It makes absolutely no sense to me to put your life at risk for your pet.

I think it's awesome that you have pets. But if they happen to get loose and run down the freeway, can we all just agree it must be their time to go?

On a very small scale, the irrational, passionate, extravagant love people have for their pets illustrates God's love for humanity. God lavishes his love on us even when we don't return it—kind of like cats.

Next to God's love, of course, the illustration falls flat. A human chasing a dog with a death wish down a freeway is nothing compared to God's crazy love for humanity. We insist on running away from God, yet God insists on running toward us. It is inexplicable.

The major theme of the Bible is that God's love passionately pursues humankind. If all you ever heard from the Bible were a bunch of dos and don'ts, then that statement might surprise you. But no matter who we are, where we are, or what we think about God, he is madly in love with us. The Bible says he knows every detail about our lives. David, an amazing songwriter and poet, wrote an entire psalm about this (Psalm 139). God knows our thoughts, our actions, and even the number of hairs on our heads. He loves to follow our lives. He watches us when we sleep—which sounds creepy but is actually comforting if you stop and think about it. He is there when we awake in the morning, and he has good things planned for us during the day.

God has no ulterior motive in all of this. He isn't some sort of control freak, trying to manipulate us or bribe us or intimidate us into holiness. He genuinely loves us and wants the best for our lives. When the Bible talks about the dangers of sin, it is simply to help us avoid pitfalls and get the most out of our lives. It's not for God's sake—it's for ours.

If we would stop scampering down the freeway and take a look back, we'd see God in hot pursuit. Not to punish or berate us, but to rescue and embrace us. And maybe to take us back to the spa.

God values us for who we are—no conditions, no caveats, no fine print.

Sometimes we might think that God is just interested in our behavior, like a cosmic policeman watching and waiting for us to slip up. We might think he almost enjoys punishing people. After all, we've known a few authority figures who got a kick out of wielding their power, and maybe God is the same, only infinitely more so.

To make things worse, we know we have issues and weaknesses and dark corners that no one sees. Being loved by God can seem far out of reach. Sometimes we are afraid that if we get close to God, we will be exposed for who we really are.

We long to be loved and to love, but we feel unlovable. And our knowledge of our neediness makes us hide from God, the one who loves us the most. Because we think if he sees us for who we really are, he's just going to get angry. So we walk around with plastic smiles, but inside we're held together with duct tape and baling wire.

I don't mean to paint an overly bleak picture here—I'm sure

many or even most of us experience genuine love from family and friends. But deep inside, I think we often want more. We want to know that we are important, that we are valuable, that we are loved.

God is the best source—dare I say the only source?—of the true love we are all looking for. Human love is wonderful and important and necessary, but it pales in comparison to the power of God's love to satisfy our souls and heal our hearts.

God loves us with never-ending love and unconditional passion. He longs to gather us in his arms—not to criticize or control or condemn, but simply to love us, to heal us, to restore us.

God's love chases us; and the sooner it catches us, the better.

True Love

Human beings are fascinated and consumed and enthralled by the idea of true love.

One of my generation's classic movies is *The Princess Bride.* Who doesn't remember the Rodents of Unusual Size, or Andre the Giant, or Inigo Montoya saying, "You killed my father. Prepare to die"?

Anyway, thanks to that movie, I can't say "true love" without hearing the whole wedding scene from *The Princess Bride* in my head. "Mawage. Mawage is wot bwings us together today. Mawage, that bwessed awangement, that dweam within a dweam . . . And wuv, tru wuv, will fowow you foweva . . ."

Actually, true love is the theme of the whole movie. Remember the old woman who yells at Princess Buttercup for betraying Wesley? "Your true love lives. And you marry another!" Then she mocks the crowd: "Bow to her. Bow to the Queen of Slime, the Queen of Filth, the Queen of Putrescence. Boo! Boo! Rubbish. Filth. Slime. Muck. Boo! Boo! Boo!"

And of course, there was Miracle Max: "Sonny, true love is the greatest thing in the world—except for a nice MLT: mutton, lettuce, and tomato sandwich, where the mutton is nice and lean and the tomato is ripe."

I could go on, but I won't. Here's my point. True love is not only the theme of *The Princess Bride*, but it is arguably the theme of life itself. Can you think of anything more important? Just look at pop culture. Look at our movies, songs, and books. Look at what occupies our thoughts and conversations. Love is the theme of life.

It's no coincidence that as humans we are consumed with the idea of love; God is consumed with love. When it comes to God, love isn't just an action—it's a state of existence. God is love. It is one of the main characteristics that make him who he is. Not all love is God, and love is not the god we worship. But God is love personified.

God created us to love and be loved. This desire, this attraction, this magnetic pull toward love is hardwired into us.

We will never be satisfied in life without love. Friendship, flirting, romance, marriage, sex, family—our lives are defined and directed and designed around love.

God created human beings out of a desire for relationship.

He created Adam and Eve because he wanted to love and be loved. That was his dream from the beginning, and nothing has changed. He is still a God who values love above everything.

So he created a garden called Eden. It was a utopia and a paradise where God and humanity could be together. Adam and Eve were perfect companions and teammates. They were meant to enjoy each other in this garden. They had fruit trees, they lived on waterfront property, they had plenty of pets, they were in love, they were naked—hello!—and there was no jealousy or shame or conflict. They were the centerpieces of God's creation.

Everything was going great until Adam and Eve did the one thing God told them not to do: eat from a certain tree in the garden. They were in the middle of the most amazing, awe-inspiring, pleasure-filled environment, and they went for the only thing that was off-limits.

Now, you might ask, "Why did God put the tree there in the first place? Why didn't he simply make it impossible to dis-obey him?"

Love by definition requires the ability to choose. If we can't choose to love or not to love, then we really can't say we love at all. God didn't want a planet full of robots hardwired to obey him. Love had to have free will—a choice.

The opposite of love is not hate; it is selfishness. Adam and Eve chose self over love. They chose self over God.

Selfishness is the essence of sin. Think about it: How much of the pain and suffering in the world is not caused by natural disasters or by accidents, but by humans willfully pursuing their own desires? If we could simply follow the golden rule, to treat others the way we would want to be treated, imagine what would happen to much of the evil in the world.

But let's face it: We don't often choose the golden rule, especially if it's going to cost us something. We admire the idea of love, but selfishness is so ingrained in us that it usually wins out. Even our pursuits of love tend to be selfish—then we wonder why love doesn't work out so well.

God granted Adam and Eve free will, and they chose sin. Paradise and perfection were compromised, and now there is a division and a chasm between man and God called sin. It is a chasm caused by man's own choice of self, but God didn't let that stop him.

God is just, and sin had to be dealt with. He couldn't sweep it under the rug. But first and foremost God is love, so he couldn't just wipe out humanity and start over, either. So he solved the problem of sin once and for all by sending his son, Jesus, to take the punishment for our sin. Jesus went to the cross to pay the penalty for every evil deed that the human race has ever committed. Justice was served, and humanity was rescued.

Think about the contrast between Adam's selfishness and Jesus' love. Adam chose self and sin, and through his selfishness, evil entered the world. Jesus chose love over self and, through his love, the power of sin and evil was destroyed.

The entire Bible is the story of God's love for humanity. It is not about sin, or about performance, or about religion; it is about a God who incessantly, obsessively, relentlessly loves his creation and went to great lengths to restore people to himself.

Here's how one verse—probably the most famous verse in the Bible—puts it: "For God so loved the world that He gave His only begotten Son, that whoever believes in Him should not perish but have everlasting life." If you haven't watched a football game lately, that's John 3:16.

John 3:16 was written, logically enough, by a guy named John. John was one of Jesus' closest disciples. We'll talk about his unique relationship with Jesus later, but let me just say he is called the Apostle of Love for a reason. Of all the disciples, he was the one who seems to have best understood God's love.

Toward the end of his life, decades after Jesus' death and resurrection, John wrote a letter we now know as 1 John. In chapter 4, verse 10, he says, "This is real love—not that we loved God, but that he loved us and sent his Son as a sacrifice to take away our sins" (NLT).

This is real love. This is true love. Not that we loved God—we didn't, and even now we aren't always the best at loving him—but that God gave the best of himself to save the worst of us. We had done nothing to earn or deserve his love, but he extravagantly and unconditionally lavished his love on the whole world.

Marry a Prostitute

About 750 years before Jesus was born, there was an Israelite prophet named Hosea. In that culture, a prophet was someone who heard from God and then shared God's message with the people. Hosea had a lot to say about the nature of love, especially God's love.

One day, God comes to Hosea and tells him that instead of a message, he has an assignment for him. Hosea is going to be an object lesson, and his personal life is about to become very public. The story is found in the first chapter of the book named after Hosea.

God says, "Hosea, I've got a job for you. Are you ready?"

Hosea is like, "Sure, God! You and me working together—this is going to be fun."

"Marry a prostitute."

"I'm sorry, Lord; what was that? I could have sworn I heard you say . . ."

"Marry a prostitute."

"Um, wow. That's what I thought you said. No offense, but that's not what I expected. That's not really a good move for a man of God. The tabloids and stuff, they're going to be all over that. Now my PR guy says that I should—"

"Hosea, you're going to marry a prostitute. And you're going to have kids."

So Hosea stops whining and marries a prostitute with the odd-sounding name of Gomer. Hosea and Gomer don't live happily ever after, unfortunately. Not even close.

I should mention that at the time, Israel's definition of love was very dysfunctional. If you read the book of Hosea, you'll see this reflected in Hosea's messages. The people of the day viewed love as a commodity that could be purchased. They also saw love as the pursuit of self-gratification. And finally, they spoke of loving inanimate objects.

This was how they defined love: you can buy it, it's about being satisfied personally, and it's about possessions and things.

Sounds a lot like our culture today.

God recognizes that he must demonstrate to them what love really is. So he tells Hosea, "Go marry a prostitute."

Hosea marries Gomer, and things go pretty well at first. They have one kid, then another, then another. They've been married awhile now. One day Hosea wakes up and she is gone. She's abandoned the family and returned to prostitution.

Hosea is now carrying the weight of being the spiritual leader of Israel as a single dad with three kids.

This brings us to Hosea, chapter 3. God says to Hosea, "Go again, love a woman who is loved by a lover and is committing adultery." He is referring to Gomer.

"What?" Hosea asks in disbelief.

"Go find Gomer. Go love this woman who is right now committing adultery. Go find your wife and love her."

And then God makes one of the most amazing statements ever. He tells Hosea to love Gomer "just like the love of the Lord" for his people. God is saying that his love is not like ours. Against all common sense, in contrast to our human ideas about justice and commitment, God's love never quits.

How heart wrenching is this process for Hosea? He has to go look for his wife, a former prostitute, who is now back in prostitution. Finding Gomer is not comfortable. It's not neat or tidy. He walks down streets and goes into buildings that good people avoid. A man of God should never be seen there; everyone knows that.

But there goes Hosea, looking for his wife. This is illogical. This is unfair. This is extravagant. He should never have to do this.

It gets more unbelievable. Verse 2 says, "So I bought her for myself for fifteen shekels of silver."

Wait! What? She was his wife. Why is he paying for her?

Somehow, Gomer has become trapped in the sex slave industry. Evidently she left Hosea voluntarily, but now she finds herself captive.

Does Hosea find her on some pedestal somewhere, chained and shackled, beaten, on sale to the highest bidder? Hosea sees his wife, the mother of their three children, and he tells her seller, "Excuse me, sir, that's my wife."

The man says, "I don't care who you think she is, this is her price."

"But I . . . But she . . . All right. I understand. What's the price?"

Hosea pays the money and receives his wife. Can you imagine that exchange? When Hosea looks into the eyes of his wife?

No doubt she hangs her head in embarrassment. She expects rejection. She expects rebuke. Gomer knows what it is like to be purchased by men who want to use her. That has been the story of her life. It is what she thinks she deserves. But Hosea doesn't buy her to use her. He buys her to heal her.

She has to wonder: *He's found me—and now he's buying*

me? I abandoned him. I abandoned our three kids. And yet he insists on buying me back? What kind of a man is this?

Verse 3 tells us what Hosea says to his wife next. This blows my mind, because I can't imagine myself saying this if I were him. "You are to live with me many days; you must not be a prostitute or be intimate with any man, and I will behave the same way toward you" (NIV).

What is he doing? He is renewing their vows. He is restoring their relationship. She probably can't even look up, but he is making their marriage as if she had never wronged him.

Interestingly, the name Hosea means "salvation" in Hebrew, and the name Gomer means "completion." I don't think that's a coincidence. God is preaching the gospel 750 years before Jesus. He is telling his people that in the middle of their rebellion and stubborn sin, he will complete their salvation. No matter how far they have strayed, he will take the initiative to find them, heal them, and love them.

So Hosea is a picture of God and—no offense—Gomer is a picture of you and me.

God created humankind. We are his. But we left him, so to speak, through sin. Humanity turned its back on God and insisted on going its own way.

And yet, two thousand years ago, God paid a dear price to redeem us from sin. He paid for what was already his, and his Son, Jesus, spilled his blood to buy us back.

Our Hosea has come. Salvation has come. He found you and he found me. He had to walk in the most despicable places and he had to roam the darkest alleys to find the people he so passionately loves. As Hosea searched for his wife, so Jesus came searching for the salvation of humanity.

And by the way, when God found us, we were not so neat and nice and put together as maybe we are now. We were in chains. We were naked, sinful, and helpless. And our gracious God said, "How much? Very well. I'll send my Son, Jesus."

You're Gomer. I'm Gomer. We were bent on following our own plans, our own will, and it only got us stuck in sin. But God didn't let that stop him. He wouldn't rest until he found us.

Maybe you've been looking for love in all the wrong places, and you're tired, and you're dirty, and you're ashamed, and you're hanging your head. God is still madly in love with you. His love is not altered by who you are or where you've been or who you were with last night. He wants you to drop your defenses and accept his embrace. His love is real. He doesn't want you for what you can do—he wants you for you.

God loves the world—and God loves you—with an uncontainable, indescribable, tireless love. His love makes life work right. It finds you and it heals you. It chases you and embraces you.

When you discover God's love, everything changes.

2

Illogical Love

God the Groupie

I recently had the terrifying privilege of observing groupies in action.

The word *groupie* is maybe not the best word for these people, but you know who I'm talking about: passionate, over-the-top fans who will go to any length to show their devotion. I was at a couple of different venues, watching entertainment figures perform, and swarms of these peculiar beings were also in attendance.

Now I don't mean to call anyone out here, but I've noticed the majority of these groupies are not of the male gender. This is just my observation, you understand; I'm not being sexist. Guys are typically not groupies because we have massive egos. It's a pride issue. So I'm not putting anyone down here. I sense some of you glaring.

Anyway, these celebrities have a passionate, devoted

following. Millions of people follow their every move. If one of these entertainment idols tweets, "I just ate Doritos #hungry," instantly thousands swoon and take to social media to declare, "OMG, I love Doritos too! It's a sign! #hungryforyou #marryme." And for two weeks, grocery stores everywhere are sold out of Doritos.

The craziest part is that girls—dare I say, women?—all over the world are convinced that they're going to marry their celebrity crushes. There are even Christian women who feel like God is intervening in the equation; they think he has spoken to them that they are destined to marry that particular person. Well, okay. Who am I to argue with God?

This is what groupies do. It's who they are. They can't help themselves. They travel, they follow, they watch, they love, and they believe that someday, somewhere, at some concert, the object of their devotion will catch their eye, they will catch his eye, and the doctrine of Walt Disney will be fulfilled—they will live happily ever after.

Most of us would probably not see this as healthy behavior. And if we had a minute to appeal to one of these young ladies, one of these fangirls, we would say, "Hold on, young lady. Look at yourself. You're intelligent. You're beautiful. You're amazing. Let it go!"

"Let what go?" she would say.

"Let him go!"

"Who?"

"That guy whose face is plastered all over your bedroom wall!"

"No, not him!"

"Yes—he will never love you!"

"You don't know that!"

"I'm pretty sure though!"

Enjoying his music and thinking he's kind of cute—that's great. But there's a world of difference between that and saying she wants to marry him and love him forever and forever. The hard reality is that he will never reciprocate her feelings. It's not going to happen.

That's what most of us would try to say. "It's not healthy. It's not good for you. Your heart is going to be crushed because it's never going to happen."

And a certain demographic would chime in and try to talk some sense into her. "Friend, grow up. This is not going to work. Trust me, I know. Donnie from New Kids on the Block— we never got together. It's not going to happen for you either."

It's not healthy. It's not good. So we say, and maybe we're right.

God Loves the World

We looked at John 3:16 in the last chapter. It's worth repeating: "For God so loved the world that He gave His only begotten Son, that whoever believes in Him should not perish but have everlasting life." Do you see that? God is the biggest groupie ever. His obsession with us is almost embarrassing.

Everyone thinks this is such a nice verse, and it is

nice—but it starts off with an astronomical, illogical, ridiculous opening phrase: "God so loved the world." Have you ever stopped to think about the implications of that phrase?

It doesn't say, "God loved some of the world." It doesn't say, "God loved those who loved him back." It simply says, "God so loved the world."

God loves the world. And if you just read that without feeling a bit uncomfortable, you read it too fast. God loves the whole world? This doesn't make sense. This is crazy. What about bad people? What about indifferent people? What about those who mock him to his face, who flaunt their evil and flout his commands?

Consider for a moment how out of control God's love for the world is. God knows everything. He is outside of time and space, and he knows what is going to happen before it happens. I can't fully explain this, but God knows who will love him and receive him, yet he chooses to love the whole world. Indiscriminately. Recklessly. Stubbornly.

God doesn't distinguish between people who love him and people who hate him, at least not in the sense that it affects his love for them. He doesn't love good people more and bad people less. His love is unconditional. It is based on who he is, not on who we are or what we do.

God's love is constant, unchanging, unrelenting. He will never love us more than he does now, and he will never love us less. Compared to God's crazy, illogical love for people who will never notice him, never respond to him, and never love him back, fangirls are emotional flatliners.

Some of us would like to give God some advice from our hard-earned life experiences. "But God," we would tell him, "this is not good. This is not normal or healthy or logical. You are obsessed with these people. You watch their every move. You follow them on Twitter. You stalk them on Facebook. You read *People* magazine. God! Stop! They are never going to acknowledge you. They are never going to know you. They are never going to love you.

"This isn't good for you, God! It makes sense that you would love me. And I reciprocate. But this whole idea of you loving everybody—it's not good. You need to be a bit more selective with your feelings and your emotions. How can you waste your love like that? You need to be careful. You need to be cautious. You shouldn't get so emotionally involved with impossible causes."

As humans, we typically do not do well when our affection is not returned. We are reciprocal beings. Mutual response is critical to a loving relationship.

If my wife, Chelsea, and I are on a date, and she is pouring out her feelings to me but I am busy catching up on my Instagram feed—trust me, things are not going to go well for me, and rightfully so.

Sure, there are times we love blindly, but only to a point. Somewhere along the line, if the object of our love ignores us or rejects us long enough, our love turns to indifference or even hate.

But not God. He is obsessed with us, and nothing we can do will ever change that.

I'll Come Back to That

The Bible says in the second chapter of the book of 1 Timothy that God "wants everyone to be saved and to understand the truth. For there is only one God and one Mediator who can reconcile God and humanity—the man Christ Jesus. He gave his life to purchase freedom for everyone" (NLT).

Jesus died to purchase freedom for everyone. Think about that for a second. We read over it so quickly, but it's crazy. If you knew those who would accept and reject you, why would you die for everyone?

On the cross, Jesus took the punishment for all sins. His suffering was not just nails, or a crown of thorns, or whippings on his back. The greatest agony and the greatest pain was that Jesus became sin. He became every sin that would ever be committed.

If I were God, and if my son were voluntarily carrying the weight and punishment for the sins of humanity, I would only put upon him the sins of those who would accept the sacrifice. Otherwise, it's a waste. Why add to the suffering by having him die for people who would never respond to the agony he is going through on their behalf?

But Jesus bore the punishment for all sins that would ever be committed by every human being that would ever live. Why?

There is only one explanation: love. It is love on such an irrational, illogical level that we should probably write ". . ." after it, because God's love doesn't conclude. It doesn't resolve.

It doesn't have closure. We can't fully understand it or describe it. The best we can do is put *dot, dot, dot* after it.

Back when I was a senior taking freshman math—which is another story for another time—if I didn't understand something, I'd think to myself, *I'll skip it for now, but I'll come back to that.* So I'd skip it and go to the next problem. But then I wouldn't understand that one either. So I'd skip it too. *I'll come back to that.*

Eventually I'd run out of problems to go to. It didn't do me any good to "come back to that" because it was still beyond my understanding. I just couldn't grasp why math—which is supposed to be about numbers—would have letters in it. Whose idea was that?

No matter how many times we look at the love of God, we can never fully understand it. It's more incomprehensible than algebra, quantum physics, rocket science, and feminine intuition put together.

God loves the world. I'll spend the rest of my life trying to understand that.

3

Love Leads

Start with the End

I don't know what it is about human beings, but we love clichés. We love reducing complex problems to cute sayings and pithy thoughts. Maybe it reinforces our illusion of control or something.

We pass these clichés down through the generations. I find myself doing this as a dad. "Son, what doesn't kill you makes you stronger." Well, sure, but what doesn't kill you still hurts.

Or how about this one: "No pain, no gain"? That's depressing. My dad's motto was, "No pain, no pain." I'm for that one, actually. I really like that one.

One of my first collisions with someone who lived by a cliché happened when I was a senior in high school. A teacher mentioned that his favorite Bible verse was, "God helps those who help themselves." I didn't have the heart to tell him that's actually not in the Bible. It's just a cliché.

There's one cliché I actually like. It's simple but genuinely profound: "Always start with the end in mind." A related one is, "It's not how you start, but how you finish." These two clichés actually hold a lot of wisdom for life.

When you are thinking about starting something, it's always good to ask yourself, *Where is this going to end?* Then, based on where you want to end up, you can start appropriately. It's about sustainability, it's about consistency, and it's about finishing well.

When you have a few kids, you start thinking about the end. Not "ending it all"—that's not what I'm saying. That shoe might fit, but that's not where I was heading. When you start raising kids, you find yourself asking, *What is the end result of my parenting going to be? Am I doing this right? Am I making the right calls? If I buy them Krispy Kreme donuts right now, will I ruin their lives forever?* If you're a parent, you know what I'm talking about.

We should think about this not just in relationship to our kids, but to our own lives as well. How are we going to turn out? What do we want to be known for? What do we want engraved on our tombstones? In other words, we need to decide what we're going to live for and what we're going to die for.

I think most of us, once we get an honest look at our own mortality and finiteness, would agree that life is about more than just making ourselves happy. It's about more than money, or fame, or sex, or power, or pleasure. If you've been sucking oxygen on Earth for long at all, you've probably figured out that those things don't last very long and they aren't very satisfying anyway. They aren't bad, of course—they are good in the right context—but they don't deserve to be enshrined as our lifelong purpose.

If we believe in God, and if we believe that he loved us enough to send his Son, Jesus, so that we could be forgiven, then the next logical step is to realize that life points to God. It is our relationship to him that gives our lives significance and solidity.

When I die, I don't want to be known for my political persuasion. I don't want to be known for some invention. I don't want to be known for an organization that I built.

When I die, I want to be known as a man who knew Jesus, enjoyed Jesus, was loved by Jesus, and focused on Jesus. When my loved ones write something on my tombstone, I want it to have to do with Jesus. I want my life to end there, so I want my life to start there.

The problem is, there is nothing within me that can guarantee I will continue to follow Jesus. I'm not smart enough, self-disciplined enough, or holy enough to make it through life without getting distracted by selfishness and sin. I might try my best to be faithful to God and to do what's right, but I know I'm only human. I know I will fail.

Last Man Standing

I'm not the first person in the universe to struggle with this, of course. Anyone who has tried to do what is right knows how frustrating it can be. We make grandiose promises about how we are going to live for God, but then we find ourselves failing within the hour.

There is a story toward the end of Jesus' time on earth that illustrates how we can make sure that at the end of our lives, we will be where we want to be—close to Jesus.

Remember John, whom we looked at in a previous chapter? Toward the end of his biography of Jesus—the Gospel of John—he describes the most famous dinner party ever: the Last Supper. It's called the Last Supper because this was the final meal Jesus had with his twelve disciples before he died on the cross.

These young men believed that Jesus was a political savior who would lead Israel to freedom from Rome. They expected him to somehow overthrow Rome and restore the national kingdom of Israel. Given that Rome wouldn't be too excited to hear about an uprising, and given that the Pharisees and other religious leaders of the day were insanely jealous of Jesus' popularity, tensions were probably a bit high during dinner.

In chapter 13, John describes what happened toward the end of the meal:

When Jesus had said these things, He was troubled in spirit, and testified and said, "Most assuredly, I say to you, one of you will betray Me."

Then the disciples looked at one another, perplexed about whom He spoke.

Now there was leaning on Jesus' bosom one of His

disciples, whom Jesus loved. Simon Peter therefore motioned to him to ask who it was of whom He spoke.

Then, leaning back on Jesus' breast, he said to Him, "Lord, who is it?"

Jesus answered, "It is he to whom I shall give a piece of bread when I have dipped it." And having dipped the bread, He gave it to Judas Iscariot, the son of Simon. (verses 21–26)

You might have noticed this passage mentions Jesus' *bosom* and his *breast*, which are not exactly masculine terms anymore. But they are important to our story, so I'll explain why they are there. In plain English, this was his chest; but in the Jewish culture these terms were symbolic of care, fellowship, and intimacy. Back then people ate at low tables, reclining on cushions. So the "disciple whom Jesus loved" was basically leaning on Jesus while they ate. Today this would be awkward and a definite invasion of personal space, but back then it was just a sign of close friendship.

In case you haven't guessed it, John himself was "the disciple Jesus loved." He refers to himself this way five times in the book of John. I think it's awesome—John defined himself by Jesus' love. It almost sounds pompous, but it wasn't. He was just 100 percent certain of Jesus' love for him. The other disciples probably read his book later on and were like, "Good grief, John! Why do you always say that? He loved all of us." John just lived life as if he were Jesus' favorite. I think that's a great way to live.

So they are all eating this meal together, and Jesus drops a bombshell. He says one of them is going to betray him.

Keep in mind that, just hours earlier, all the disciples had promised to stay faithful to Jesus no matter what—even to death. The conversation is recorded in the fourteenth chapter of the Gospel of Mark, verses 27–31:

On the way, Jesus told them, "All of you will desert me. For the Scriptures say,

'God will strike the Shepherd,
     and the sheep will be scattered.'

But after I am raised from the dead, I will go ahead of you to Galilee and meet you there."
Peter said to him, "Even if everyone else deserts you, I never will."
Jesus replied, "I tell you the truth, Peter—this very night, before the rooster crows twice, you will deny three times that you even know me."
"No!" Peter declared emphatically. "Even if I have to die with you, I will never deny you!" And all the others vowed the same. (NLT)

Of all the disciples, Peter tends to be the one who talks the most. "Even if everyone else deserts you, I never will!" And he meant it. He really did. But a few hours later, when Jesus is arrested and taken, all the disciples flee. And Peter denies Jesus three different times, just as Jesus said he would.

Now let's look at the end. In John, chapter 19, verses 25–27, we see Jesus on the cross:

> Standing near the cross were Jesus' mother, and his mother's sister, Mary (the wife of Clopas), and Mary Magdalene. When Jesus saw his mother standing there beside the disciple he loved, he said to her, "Dear woman, here is your son." And he said to this disciple, "Here is your mother." And from then on this disciple took her into his home. (NLT)

At the end, John is right beside the cross. Right beside the person whose love meant everything to him. The Bible doesn't tell us where the other disciples were. They might not have been at the cross at all.

Peter, in particular, is noticeably absent. After vehemently betraying Jesus for the third time, we read in Luke, chapter 22, that when he remembered what Jesus told him, he "went out and wept bitterly." So while John is at the foot of the cross, Peter is out somewhere fixated on his failures. Not to be judgmental, but this wasn't the best time for a pity party. If ever Jesus needed loyalty and friendship, it was now. But Peter—who had sworn his faithfulness to Jesus more than anyone—is nowhere to be found.

What was it about John that led him to be, as far as we know, the only disciple at the foot of the cross? What did his start look like, and how did it lead him toward the end that he desired? And what was it about Peter that ended up sabotaging him? After all, both John and Peter loved Jesus and wanted to do what was right. Why is John remembered for being at the cross and Peter for denying Jesus publicly?

The answers to these questions teach us how we can remain faithful to God to the end.

John Versus Peter

Go back to the scene in John, chapter 13, known as the Last Supper. When I read this passage, I feel like I'm watching a movie, and the camera keeps cutting back and forth between the main characters. Most people would say Judas is one of the main characters here, but actually the real stars are Jesus, Peter, and John. You'll notice the camera zeroes in on them more than once.

Jesus says someone in the room is going to betray him. They all gasp. They start to panic and look at each other. The camera goes to a close-up of John and shows him just lounging beside Jesus. He's not really doing anything but sitting there, leaning on Jesus.

Then it cuts to Peter. Peter is doing what most of us would do. He is frantically motioning, trying to figure out who the bad guy is. My guess is that his motions involve a lot of pointing—"Is it him? Or is it him? Or how about him?" That would be classic Peter, wouldn't it? I know it's what I would do.

Danger is imminent, and Peter is up in arms. He has to do something. He has to find out who the traitor is. He has to fix things.

I can relate to that. When painful or difficult things come up in my life, my knee-jerk reaction isn't to lie around like John. It's to jump up like Peter and do something. When there's a challenge in your business or family or health, your gut reaction is probably not to use Jesus as a pillow, right? You want to do something.

There are ten other disciples, including Judas, but we don't hear much about them. Why does the Bible take the time to compare and contrast these two characters? I think God is telling us something just by the physical postures and reactions of these two men.

Interesting note: Peter's name means "stone," which is what the Ten Commandments were written on. John's name means "the Lord is gracious." I think we can see a contrast here between law and love.

Peter is active, working, striving. That's just what happens in life when someone trusts in him- or herself to fulfill God's commandments. It's a life lived by stone, by the law. We work it out and make it happen. It's about performance. It's about action.

This is Peter's propensity, and it's often ours as well. When the rubber meets the road, when push comes to shove, when the heat gets turned up (wow, the clichés are coming to me now) we have to *do* something. So we send the e-mail, make the phone call, call the meeting.

What's John's problem? Come on, John. Jesus is hurting here. He's in a lot of pain, and you're using him as a pillow. John, aren't you going to do anything? Do you need some Red Bull or a triple grande latte or something?

But who was at the foot of the cross at the crucifixion? Just John. Peter was painfully absent.

Here's my point. John understood what it meant to live in the love of Jesus. He knew how to rest his head on Jesus' heart even when chaos and uncertainty and fear were the order of the day. He was "the disciple Jesus loved." The love of Jesus was his identity, his focus, his priority. Love was how he started and how he lived his life, and love led him to finish well.

John didn't rely on his brawn and brains and bravery like Peter did. He didn't seem to think he had to fix everything. He knew that true security and strength were found not in frantic human effort, but in resting in Jesus' love.

Magnetic Love

It's interesting to note that it wasn't just Peter who didn't live up to his vow to be loyal. The Bible says all the disciples made the same promise. That includes John—he promised, and he failed.

But there was something about John's relationship with Jesus that went deeper than his promises and his performance. It was something that enabled him to overcome his failures almost instantly and rush back to Jesus' side when it counted the most.

It was love.

And I would say, based on what I read in John's writings, that it wasn't so much John's love for Jesus that drew him back. It was Jesus' love for John. Even in his weakness and his failures and his fears, John was able to return to the foot of the cross because his mind was more consumed with Jesus' love for him than with his own love—or lack of love—for Jesus.

Peter was MIA because he was a casualty of condemnation. If we live by the law, we die by the law. If our whole focus is how much *we* can do for God, how devoted *we* are to him, and how much *we* love him—rather than how much *he* does for us and how much *he* loves us—eventually we'll find ourselves in a pity party apart from the cross.

Faithfulness and hard work and commitment are great—don't get me wrong—but we can't put our trust in ourselves. We can't depend on our own efforts and self-discipline to stay true to Jesus.

It sounds so spiritual and so right to make flamboyant vows about our commitment to God, but vows won't keep us at the foot of the cross. Only love will. Keeping ourselves in the love of God is the way to end well.

John filtered everything through God's love for him. Problems couldn't stop him. Threats couldn't stop him. Condemnation and guilt couldn't stop him. He was magnetically drawn to Jesus because he had a habit of letting love lead.

Life is not easy at times. The problems we face are real. And for most of us, our tendency is to jump up and get to work. We want to fix things, change things, make things happen. But sometimes we forget to let God's love lead.

I'll be honest: more often than not, I look a little like John, but a lot more like Peter. When things are good, I'm pretty good at leaning on Jesus. But when painful news comes, when danger is in the mix, I want to jump up off Jesus' chest and fix things.

It's not wrong to do what is in our power to make things right. I'm not advocating laziness or irresponsibility. But our lives must start and end with a dependence on God. They must start and end in the love and grace and mercy of God. Everything else will flow from that.

God loves us. That is not a cliché. It is a powerful, unchanging reality that we can build our lives on.

Sometimes we think that what is most important to our success is our effort, our work, and our ability to follow God. Those things are great, but they aren't enough to sustain us through the chaos and craziness of life.

But the love of God is.

The only way we're going to make it over the long haul is to do what seems so counterintuitive: to lean into Jesus' love, to sit with him, recline on him, and trust in him. Let love lead your life, and you'll end well.

4

Love Gives

Dishonest Underwear

I recently discovered the miraculous undergarments known as Spanx. That's right—Spanx. If my honesty makes you uncomfortable, well, it's only going to get worse.

I wear Spanx, but let me explain. I came across this magical undergarment very innocently.

I'm a little bit OCD in some areas. One thing that drives me crazy is that I feel like I have pointy pecs—again, I'm just being honest here. I jog on the treadmill, I do pushups, and I try to stay fit, but my pointy pecs make it look like I'm not in shape. All I want is a flat, muscular, Schwarzenegger chest. Is that so bad?

Apparently I had complained about this to Chelsea more than I realized, so one day she said, "You should try this undershirt. It's called Spanx."

Now I didn't know that Spanx started as tight shorts that

women wear to pretend they are four sizes smaller. No one told me that. Apparently I'm not up on my underwear trivia.

I'm a pro-undershirt guy and always have been. So I said, "Sure, I'll try it." I put on this tighter undershirt, and instantly I had the flat chest I'd always been looking for. This was unbelievable. It was like Christmas had come early for me.

So I started telling everybody about Spanx. "Have you tried these undershirts? They're amazing!"

Then I went to this particular department store that I enjoy. My friend there is the manager, and I found him and said, "Hey, bro, I need a couple more Spanx."

And he said, "Sssssspanx?" and lowered his voice and looked around, like someone might hear us. "Uh, you wear those?"

"What, you don't?"

Then I talked to a few of my friends, and they were like, "Dude, you can't be telling people you wear Spanx." Again, sorry—I wasn't in on the undergarment community, so I didn't know there was a stigma. I thought all underwear was created equal.

But then I met with this one employee at another department store who is a Spanx expert. He was on my side. He told me, "Of course you love Spanx. They promote proper posture. They keep your stomach in and your abs flexed to help you develop your abs just by wearing them. And, of course, they are moisture wicking."

The guy was talking my language. Great posture? Yes, thank you! Moisture wicking? Absolutely! Work on my abs without working on my abs? Definitely! Can I wear three at a time?

Over time, though, I began to realize that Spanx was doing me a disservice. The Spanx expert said it would promote good, healthy things like better posture, better abs, and less sweating. That would in turn create positive momentum and I would want to work out more. So I was subconsciously counting on Spanx to produce less of me—less weight, fewer bad habits, and so on.

But Spanx was lying to me.

It's one thing to lie to others, but it's another thing altogether to lie to yourself. I have a problem with this. I'd look in the mirror, not remembering that I was wearing Spanx, and I would be like, "Well helloooo, good-looking! Guess who's eating whatever they want tonight?"

Then I'd take off the Spanx, and be like, "I don't know this man!"

I was counting on Spanx to produce less of me, but somehow there was more of me.

One day I asked Chelsea, "Babe, when was I in the best shape in our marriage?" We'd been married fourteen years, and it was an honest question. I was hoping she'd say, "Right now!" but it didn't work out like that.

She said, "Probably when you were using the Perfect Pushup regularly." The Perfect Pushup, in case you don't know, is a set of rotating handles that you hold on to while you do pushups. They were created by a Navy SEAL, so they must be awesome.

Then Chelsea said, "You know what's interesting? You stopped using the Perfect Pushup right around when we discovered Spanx."

Ouch.

New Year's Emotional Suggestions

You're probably wondering what Spanx has to do with love. Let me explain the connection. Jesus said in the eighth chapter of the Gospel of Mark,

> Whoever desires to come after Me, let him deny himself, and take up his cross, and follow Me. For whoever desires to save his life will lose it, but whoever loses his life for My sake and the gospel's will save it. For what will it profit a man if he gains the whole world, and loses his own soul? Or what will a man give in exchange for his soul? (verses 34–37)

Jesus was giving people an invitation to abundant life—not just to existence, but to abundant life. The only catch is, we get life via death. It's a paradox. Jesus was saying that the way we typically think about life and satisfaction and fulfillment is backward.

He was saying that living selfishly will actually produce death. It will steal our joy, steal our fulfillment, and steal our lives. However, if we deny ourselves, take up our cross, and follow him, we find life.

Many of us have lived long enough to know that when we finally get our ideal job, when we finally get the income we wanted, when we finally have the respect we wanted—sometimes that can be one of the emptiest days of our lives. Up until that point, our emptiness was understandable. "I feel empty because I don't have that job, that corner office, that six-figure income. I don't have the husband [or the wife or the kids]. But when I have a family, the high-paying career, the vice presidency, the influence, then I won't feel like this anymore."

Then the day comes, and we get what we always wanted, and it dawns on us that this is not it. We're still the same people. Empty. Hollow. Unsatisfied.

Jesus was saying that even if we get what we want, when we want it, and how we want it, we'll miss out on true life. We won't find lasting satisfaction. Selfishness is never the path to happiness. It is actually a very real obstacle to living the abundant life God offers us through Jesus.

I'm not saying we should lose sight of our goals and desires and aspirations. Those things are good. But we can't hang our hopes for happiness on them. If they happen, great—but if they don't, we trust that God has a better plan for us. And regardless of whether we achieve our goals or not, we are continually kept in the love of God, enraptured with his plan and his person and all that he's done for us. We will enjoy our goals, our influence, and our income far more when our satisfaction is settled and our fulfillment is found in the love of Jesus.

So if selfishness produces death and dissatisfaction, what produces life? The answer is true, unconditional, sacrificial love. This is what this passage describes.

Notice why we lose our lives, according to the passage we just read: "for My sake and the gospel's." Jesus is saying that the motive to lose our lives is essentially love. We consider Jesus; we consider the people who need to know about his love, his goodness, his mercy, his story, and his salvation; and we are internally motivated to give our lives. We lose our self-based lives and find true life in him.

Love is the opposite of selfishness. Love gives; selfishness takes. Love thinks about others; selfishness thinks about itself.

The problem is that, as human beings, we are not naturally loving, giving, and generous. We are selfish. Don't take that personally; it's human nature. We tend to be self-focused and self-absorbed. We were born that way. We have to learn to love and give and serve.

Here's where the Spanx effect comes in.

When we read passages like this, we often inadvertently lie to ourselves. We think, *Okay, it says to deny yourself. If I'm going to follow Jesus and if I'm going to find this life he's talking about, then I have to deny myself. I have to take up my cross. I have to forget about myself and what I need and what I want, and I have to force myself to love God and people.*

That sounds great, right? It sounds so spiritual. But if I try to deny myself all by myself, I actually focus on *self* more than ever. Emphasizing self is inherently counterproductive. Self is the problem, not the solution.

The answer to living a selfless, sacrificial, loving, giving life is not gritting our teeth and making ourselves love more. That kind of self-effort is doomed to failure. It's like wearing Spanx: I expect less of myself, but I end up with more of myself.

Our spiritual-sounding promises are similar to New Year's resolutions. Have you ever made one of those? More tellingly, have you ever kept one of those for, say, longer than a week?

Who are we kidding? Those are not resolutions. They are emotional suggestions. Give it forty-eight hours. Around January 3 we find ourselves mumbling, "Uh, never mind. I didn't really mean it."

Some people are anomalies, of course, and if you are one of these anomalies, I honor you. You are the rare find on this planet. You are disciplined, you are motivated, and you do what you say you're going to do.

The rest of us are pretty normal. And we typically don't do what we say we're going to do, especially when we say it around midnight on December 31. "I'm going to eat better this year. I'm going to work out more this year. I'm going to do push-ups instead of wearing Spanx this year."

Good luck with that. That is just discipline. That is just willpower.

We can't reduce the teachings of Jesus to a New Year's resolution. Our desire to love generously and to live a good life is commendable. But if it's based on sheer willpower, it's not going to work long-term. Self-based change is rarely sustainable or substantial, and it doesn't have the power to produce satisfaction or fulfillment in our lives.

It's Not About You

The point of this passage is not to try harder. It is to shift our focus.

If we're going to truly deny ourselves, if we are going to love and give and think about others first, then we have to be preoccupied and consumed with someone other than ourselves. Notice the wording of Jesus' invitation. He said, "If you want to come after *me*, deny yourself, take up your cross, and follow *me*." The "deny yourself" portion is bookended by the word *me*. It's framed by a focus on Jesus.

In other words, if we are interested in Jesus, if we want to love him and love like him, if we want the abundant life that is found in him, then we need to stop thinking about ourselves. We need to focus on him and his love for us.

Jesus said that if we try to hoard our lives for ourselves, we end up losing our lives. It's like trying to grasp the air. We try to get stuff and get happiness and get satisfaction, but ironically, the more we focus on ourselves, the more we lose our satisfaction, our fulfillment, and our meaning.

But when we become preoccupied and consumed and enamored with Jesus, we forget about what we want, when we want it, and how we think we can get it. We lose our lives, but we actually find them. We discover the fulfillment we desire when we stop trying to find it in and through ourselves.

What is the motivation for giving up our lives? For loving God and loving people? Is it because self-denial is noble and admirable, and we should all be disciplined people?

Wrong. That will never work.

We lose our lives because we forget ourselves as we remember and revel in the love of Jesus—in who he is and what he has done for us. We lose sight of our urges and surges, our desires and our wants. We lose sight of ourselves and we become enamored with him. We get pumped about his story, because now his story is our story. And before we know it, we're living in satisfaction and fulfillment.

Community and Carbs

In the book of Acts, the Bible gives us a description of the very first church. This was the original community of Jesus followers who started gathering together to worship. We can see in their lifestyle that they took Jesus up on his invitation. They led lives of extraordinary satisfaction predicated upon denying themselves and focusing on Jesus. And as a result, they were some of the most loving, giving people you could imagine.

By the time we pick up our story, there were thousands of people in the church, possibly around six thousand, and the community was growing every day.

We read in chapter 2, verse 42 that the people "continued steadfastly in the apostles' doctrine and fellowship, in the breaking of bread, and in prayers." Doctrine means that the disciples were telling them the teachings of Jesus. Fellowship means they were all hanging out, enjoying one another, and socializing. And they were eating carbs. I love this church! Talking about Jesus, enjoying friends, eating carbs, and praying. Who wouldn't want that?

It goes on. Verse 43 talks about awe coming upon everyone. In other words, people had a sense that God is awesome and that he was among them. It means these thousands of people had a profound consciousness of God's presence and reality and incredible goodness. It wasn't tradition, custom, or religion. It was God. It was real.

The next two verses are stunning: "Now all who believed were together, and had all things in common, and sold their possessions and goods, and divided them among all, as anyone had need."

You don't see Peter or any of the other leaders telling these brand-new Jesus followers to sell their stuff. Peter didn't get up and say, "Honestly, guys, these exotic cars are extravagant. It's too much. Sell them and get a Prius."

There was none of that. This was spontaneous. Thousands of people organically got a sense that they needed to take care of each other. "I'll sell this. I'll sell that. I'll sell the lot I was going to build my dream home on. God will take care of me. We've got to make sure everybody is taken care of."

What was happening? They were denying themselves.

Why? Because Peter did a six-week series in the church about denying yourself, so everyone was pumped?

Nope. Everyone was just really aware of Jesus. In some cases you have people who saw him, who walked with him, who lived with him. Jesus was real to them, and his reality had found its way into the hearts and souls of six thousand people. They were so aware of Jesus and his majesty and his beauty that before they knew it, they were spontaneously giving stuff away.

Verse 46 mentions them eating even more carbs. I told you I love this church. Some of us would be less grumpy and more like Jesus if we ate more carbs. (Okay, I don't know if that's entirely true, but it works for me.)

Then verse 46 says they had "gladness and simplicity of heart." You have to love these people. They were happy. They were laughing. They were telling jokes. Everyone else had road rage, but they were skipping down the street and whistling and blowing bubbles.

They weren't happy because the government was so great or the economy was so strong. Historically, they were living in unsettling times, especially as believers. And yet we find thousands of people who seem healthy, content, thrilled about life, happy to get together, and motivated to take care of each other.

They were denying themselves, and everyone was more fulfilled and satisfied and content than ever.

I love the next verse. It says they were all praising God. God was on their minds. Being loved by God and loving God was their focus. And as a natural result, they really, genuinely loved each other.

I don't know about you, but that's what I want for my life. I want to be so caught up in God's love that I stop thinking about myself. And I want to be surrounded by a community of people with the same focus, a community that builds each other up in love.

Forgiving Your Murderers

One of the leaders in this early church was a guy named Stephen. We read his story in Acts, chapter 7. Stephen was actually more of an administrative type. He had been given the job of helping distribute food to people in need. He was probably great with numbers, with details, with plans—basically everything that I am not.

Stephen was also in love with Jesus. Jesus changed Stephen's life, and he was the focus of Stephen's existence. As a result, Stephen couldn't help telling people about the good news of Jesus. He couldn't help living in love.

At the time of this story, there was tremendous persecution against Christians. Believing or teaching that Jesus was God had been deemed blasphemy, and it was punishable by death.

One day the wrong people heard Stephen talking about Jesus. They put him on trial for blasphemy. Then they formed a mob, and they began to stone him to death.

Stephen was dying, one harsh blow at a time. I can't imagine the agony or the sense of betrayal and violence. His own countrymen were killing him, and his only crime was that he loved Jesus and shared that love with others.

Moments from death, Stephen spoke his final words: "Lord, do not hold this sin against them" (verse 60 NIV). And with that, he died.

That sounds just like Jesus. One of the final things Jesus said as he was dying on the cross was "Father, forgive them, for they do not know what they do" (Luke 23:34).

I've always thought, *Well, that's what makes him God, because that's not what I would say! I wouldn't say, "Father, forgive them." I'd say, "Father, get them. Get them good. And let me watch!"*

Stephen was an administrative staff member in the

community. But he looked a lot like Jesus, didn't he? Jesus was real to this young man. Stephen was so preoccupied with the reality of Jesus and his love for hurting humanity that he used his last breath to pray for the very men who were executing him.

When I read this story, I want to cut the scene and have a retake. Only I want to rewrite the lines because this is not right. It makes all of us normal dudes look really bad.

When I see someone in the HOV lane and there's only one person in the car, I'm the guy who wants to dial the hotline and turn him in. Why? Because I like justice.

If it's Christmas and I'm in a packed line at Toys "R" Us, I want to call out the guy who cuts in line. "Excuse me, sir—yes, you—we were here first. We're all waiting our turn. What's your problem, sir? Hey, everyone—this guy is trying to cut. Manager, this guy's a cutter."

Who is this Stephen guy? He has forgotten about himself. I want to stop the story and say, "Stephen, Stephen, hold on! Those are the guys killing you. Let's think this through. We're going to rewrite the lines. Your last words are going to go something like this: 'God, send now your warrior angels, and let them with blazing swords cut off the heads of these horrible men, and let their heads roll like the rocks they throw.'"

Right? That sounds pretty poetic. I like it.

But Stephen wouldn't have said it that way even if I gave him the lines. With his last painful breath, so similar to Jesus, he said, "God, I'll see you in a minute. But I have one last prayer on this planet: I pray for the men who are murdering me. Make sure you forgive them. Don't hold this against them."

What had happened in this man's heart? It was the power of love. I'm so far from this point. But if God can do it in Stephen, he can do it in me.

It's one thing to live beyond yourself for people who have done you good. But Stephen was so preoccupied with Jesus and his love for people that in the middle of great injustice, he prayed for those who hated him.

I want to live so far beyond myself that I think about the well-being of people who are hurting me. I want Jesus to be that real to me. I want to be so enthralled and in love with him that I lose myself and find his abundant life.

So let us take our eyes off ourselves and focus on the God who loves us and is for us and is with us. Let us think of the hurting humanity around us. And just as the first church experienced gladness, generosity, satisfaction, and joy, so will we.

LIFE IS to trust God in every moment.

Often, we aren't very good at enjoying what's right in front of us. We struggle with how to live in the moment, how to appreciate the present, how to relax and rejoice in all the good things in our lives.

In my experience, this struggle is not usually a result of current problems, although of course those can play a role. Overall, our fears and anxieties are a result of not knowing what tomorrow holds.

We think, *Sure, life is pretty good now. But how do I know it will stay that way? What's around the next corner? What's over the next hill? Maybe bad news is on its way right now.*

We have no guarantee of tomorrow, so we are uneasy and unsettled today. Fear of the future makes it hard to stay satisfied with life in the present.

But what choice do we have? In an uncertain world, can we ever really relax? Isn't the responsible thing to stay alert, to stay tense, to stay poised for action? It's good and noble to be responsible, but no matter how awesome we might be at it, we still can't control life. We still can't guarantee safety, serenity, and success.

Jesus offers us a better way to live. He doesn't promise that we will live without trouble or pain—he gives us something even better. He shows us how to trust God in every moment. And in our trust, we find true life.

5

Yesterday, Today, and Forever

Greener Grass

I have an unhealthy habit of checking my phone too often. It's ridiculous, actually. Sometimes I find myself looking at it five seconds after I just checked it, because maybe in the time it took me to put it back in my pocket, someone texted me or messaged me or tagged me.

And then before I know it, I'm on Instagram, looking at photos of people I don't even know. I'm looking at what they had for breakfast or at pictures of their new puppy. And if I'm not on Instagram, I hop over to Twitter and start reading pithy, mysterious statements written by people I'll never meet.

I can be on a date with my wife, the woman of my dreams, and we're eating a gourmet meal at a fantastic restaurant (that we found, coincidentally, with a smartphone app), but I'm distracted by Joe Somebody and the fact that he is eating a two-egg scramble with mozzarella. What is wrong with me?

Why am I so addicted to living vicariously through others at the expense of enjoying the people I'm currently with and the place I currently am and what I'm currently doing?

I know I'm not alone here. You see this phenomenon everywhere: two, three, four people are sitting together, but they have their noses in their cellular devices. They are surrounded by real, living, talking people, but they're engrossed with digital personalities and experiences.

And it's not like the image we portray online is even that genuine or complete. We act as art directors of our lives via social media. The other day I was at a great hotel near the ocean, but the hotel in front of us mostly blocked the view. I found myself sticking my phone as far out of our window as possible and contorting myself into positions a gymnast would have been proud of just to take a picture that I could text to a friend. "Look where we are!"

"Wow! Amazing view!"

But it wasn't even real. Only my cell phone could enjoy that view. How much of what I'm staring at on my feeds is just a staged, cropped, and filtered version of someone else's life?

It's human nature to want to be where we're not. Smartphones and social media didn't create this tendency. "The grass is always greener on the other side" could be the mantra of the human race. While we lounge in our luscious, green, thick grass, we wonder, *Does the person next to me have slightly more luscious grass? What if their grass is blue? Is blue the new green? Wow! If only I had blue grass or pink grass. All I have is this boring green grass. Stinks to be me.*

Marketing preys on this, of course. It shows us images of sun-soaked tropical locations, and it says for only a small fortune, you, too, can spend two weeks in this glorious location.

So we endure six months of drizzle and cold and hard work in order to earn this sensational image we've been sold. Then we get there, and the first thing we look for is a Wi-Fi signal so we can see what's happening back home. Here we are in Maui, but we're wondering what's happening in Minnesota. Minnesota? Really? I have nothing against Minnesota, but if I'm in Maui, I should be enjoying Maui. Minnesota will do just fine without me.

We often view time with the same grass-is-always-greener mentality. For example, the older we get, the more we tend to relive the "good ol' days."

Remember the good ol' days? Those were the days, weren't they? No cell phones. No Twitter or Facebook or e-mail. Those were simple times, back when phones were tied to the wall and you just focused on the person you were with.

Those weren't simpler times, FYI. Those were stressful times, because nobody could get ahold of anybody. Let's face it: human nature hasn't changed. It just manifests differently.

The funny thing about memories is that they have a way of looking bigger than life. It's kind of like when you put an Instagram filter on a mediocre picture—suddenly it looks vintage and nostalgic and awesome. We subconsciously edit out the things we didn't like and just remember the rosy parts.

Or, instead of the good ol' days, we become all about *someday*. So you're single and you're thinking all the time, *Right now I'm single and I'm lonely and I'm stressed-out, but some-day I'm going to get married and it's going to be great. God, help someday come soon.*

Then it comes, and you get married, and it's fun, and the intimacy is great. But now you've got an actual job, and you have responsibilities, and you have a schedule. You have another human being that you have to coordinate with and communicate with, and you have to be home at a particular time. And sometimes you see your old friends who are still single, and you think, *Oh, the good ol' days, back when I was free as a bird. I went to the movies by myself, but I was free.*

It's human nature. We are good at missing the good ol' days, and we are good at longing for someday. But in the process, we often undervalue the importance of today.

A lot of our fulfillment and satisfaction in life comes from the simple, underrated ability to live in the moment, to enjoy the moment, to experience the moment. We live life best when we live it without regretting the past or fearing the future.

Please don't misunderstand—we should learn from the past, and we should prepare for the future. I wrote a whole chapter on starting with the end in mind (chapter 3). I'm a huge proponent of living life carefully and wisely.

But living wisely doesn't mean ignoring the present. Life does not consist of what should have happened, what might have happened, or what hopefully will happen. Life is what *is happening*—right now. The past affects and informs the present, and the future helps us decide how to live in the present, but the only moment we can actually live in is *this* moment.

That sounds great in theory. But in a world that is uncertain and unstable, a world that hands us more than our share of evil and tragedy, how do we remain stable in the present?

The Bible says in Hebrews, chapter 13, verse 8: "Jesus Christ is the same yesterday, today, and forever" (NLT). That simple statement changes the way I view my life. Jesus doesn't change.

We are works in progress. We make mistakes, we learn, we change, we grow, we keep trying. But not God.

God is perfect and awesome and wonderful and righteous. He always has been and always will be. God's constancy stabilizes our inconstant lives. The fact that he is the same yesterday, right now, and for the rest of time means that we can trust him in this moment and in every moment.

Sexy Someday

This good-ol'-days-versus-someday mentality was alive and well when Jesus walked the earth. As I mentioned, it is human nature.

In the eleventh chapter of John, we read about a man named Lazarus becoming very ill. Lazarus and his two sisters, Mary and Martha, are some of Jesus' best friends. So Mary and Martha send for Jesus, hoping he will heal their brother.

> When Jesus heard that, He said, "This sickness is not unto death, but for the glory of God, that the Son of God may be glorified through it." Now Jesus loved Martha and her sister and

Lazarus. So, when He heard that he was sick, He stayed two more days in the place where He was. (verses 4–6)

Hold on. Something here doesn't make sense. Jesus hears about the illness and he knows God wants to heal Lazarus. So he does nothing? He just hangs out for a few more days?

The situation goes from bad to worse. Lazarus ends up dying. And by the time Jesus shows up at Mary and Martha's town, Lazarus has been dead for four days.

Now Martha, as soon as she heard that Jesus was coming, went and met Him, but Mary was sitting in the house. Now Martha said to Jesus, "Lord, if You had been here, my brother would not have died. But even now I know that whatever You ask of God, God will give You."

Jesus said to her, "Your brother will rise again."

Martha said to Him, "I know that he will rise again in the resurrection at the last day."

Jesus said to her, "I am the resurrection and the life. He who believes in Me, though he may die, he shall live. And whoever lives and believes in Me shall never die. Do you believe this?"

She said to Him, "Yes, Lord, I believe that You are the Christ, the Son of God, who is to come into the world." (verses 20–27)

Jesus shows up, and Martha responds how most of us would. She looks at the past. She looks at what could have happened, what should have happened, what she expected to happen. "Lord, if you had been here, my brother would not have died."

Jesus replies, "Your brother will rise again."

Now Martha jumps to the other end of the spectrum: "I know that one day he'll rise again." In an instant, she goes from looking at the past to looking at the future. Someday her brother will live again. Someday her dreams will come true. Someday things will get better.

But she's avoiding the present. It's too painful. It's too hard to believe that her circumstances can change right now. Today. In an instant.

Her faith for the future is admirable, but Jesus wants her to understand something. He isn't just God of the past or the future. He is God of the present. He doesn't just sympathize with her pain; he wants to do right now what she can't seem to let herself imagine.

We tend to do the same thing. We wish that God would have done things differently in the past, or we hope he will someday fix things in the future. But often God wants to do something awesome and amazing and miraculous right now.

He is God of our current circumstances. He knows what we're facing, and he knew we'd be facing it long before we did. So we can embrace this day and trust God in every moment.

Sure, *someday* is sexy. It's alluring. It's full of potential. Anything could happen someday. But right now is just so . . . ordinary.

We think, *Someday, in heaven, I'm going to be happy. But*

right now, circumstances are clearly not conducive to a miracle. Right now, my life is pretty much a mess. I guess I just have to hang on until heaven.

We know that heaven is real and that God will one day make everything right again. We know that faith sometimes means just hanging in there. But just because God will some-day bring a final end to death and sin and pain doesn't mean that life has to stink right now.

I Am

Jesus said to Martha, "I am the resurrection and the life." I want to take a look at that little phrase, *I am*. This isn't the first time Jesus had said something like this.

In John 8, Jesus was having a heated discussion with the religious teachers of the day, and naturally he was win-ning. They didn't like the fact that Jesus acted and talked a lot like a divine Savior, so finally, in exasperation, they asked him, "Do you really think you are better than our forefather Abraham?"

Jesus replied: "Before Abraham was, I am."

At this point in the narrative, English majors everywhere want to call a grammar time-out. "No, no, Lord. Grammati-cally speaking, that is wrong. That's confusing. I think you meant to say, 'Before Abraham was, I *was*.' *Was* and *am*, they don't go together. You either are or you were. What are you talking about?"

Again, academics weren't exactly my strong suit. But I think if an infinite, infallible God chooses to use bad grammar, he's probably making a point. Grammar police, stand down.

It might be awkward grammatically, but it's the only correct way to express God's timeless, limitless availability and sufficiency. God simply is. He is in the present, he is in the past, and he is in the future. He always exists in present tense because he is outside of time and space. Wherever you look on the time line of humanity, God is present and active. He isn't just a memory from the past or a promise for the future: he's a real-time, present-day God.

Jesus was actually quoting from one of the greatest stories in Scripture. It's found in Exodus, chapter 3. It is the story of how a man named Moses delivered Israel from slavery in Egypt some fifteen hundred years earlier. Moses was an Israelite who had been raised in the Egyptian palace, but he fled into exile in the desert after killing an Egyptian guard who was mistreating an Israelite. He was hated by Egypt and mistrusted by Israel. He wasn't exactly a prime candidate to broker the deliverance of a nation.

One day he is out tending sheep in the desert, and God speaks to him. Actually, a random bush that is on fire speaks to him, and it turns out to be God. Odd, but God likes to stay unpredictable.

So God tells Moses, "I want you to go back to Egypt and rescue your people."

Moses starts to freak out, and frankly, I can see why. Not only is he on the Egypt's Most Wanted list, but there is no way

Pharaoh, the king of Egypt, is going to let his workforce go. Someone has to build those pyramids and sphinxes and tombs.

Moses is like, "What? Who am I to do that? Besides—I stutter. You've got the wrong man for the job. This isn't going to work, and I'm going to look like a dork."

Moses is having an identity crisis. He feels insufficient. He feels like he doesn't have enough. He can't pull this off.

Notice God's answer in verse 14. This is his antidote to Moses' anxiety. He says, "I AM WHO I AM."

I'm sure Moses is thinking, *Oh, that clears up everything, doesn't it? Like not at all.*

"Moses, this is all you need to know. I AM WHO I AM."

In the face of Moses' insecurity and identity crisis, God does *not* say, "Moses, you're great. You've got this. You're smart, and you're educated, and you've got a great beard. You'll be fine."

To solve Moses' identity crisis, God reminds Moses who God is.

I love that.

The answer to our frequent identity crises is not first and foremost focusing on who we are, but focusing on who God is.

God is essentially saying, "Moses, I've got you covered. I am here. I am available. I have all the supply and surplus you could ever need. I am self-existent. I have no beginning and no end. I just am."

That changes everything.

When Jesus says to Martha, "I am the resurrection and the life," he is reminding her that he is all she really needs. In her grief and desperation, Jesus is the answer. His "I am" is more than enough for her "I need."

Roll It Away

After Jesus talks to Martha in John 11, Mary comes to him and says essentially the same things Martha did. Jesus is clearly moved with compassion when he sees their pain. Verse 35 is one of the most beautiful verses in the Bible as well as the shortest: "Jesus wept."

Even though God is infinite, timeless, and perfect, he feels our pain. He knows what he is going to do to fix it, but he still weeps with us, mourns with us, and suffers with us.

Then Jesus heads to the tomb. "Roll the stone away."

Martha is like, "But Jesus—it's been four days. Not to be gross, but it's going to smell pretty bad."

"Roll it away."

"Are you serious? Are we doing this?"

"Right now. Roll it away."

Up until the very last minute, Martha seems to have trouble believing that what she really wants is actually happening. She seems to be afraid. Afraid to hope; afraid to trust; afraid to believe. And here's the best part: Jesus raises Lazarus from the dead anyway.

We have a tendency to allow fear to short-circuit what God wants to do, but God can do what he wants, when he wants to do it. He doesn't even need our faith, our spirituality, our good works, or our permission to do it. He is God, and he operates by grace.

Sometimes we are so painfully aware of our own limitations that we project those limitations on God. God is not limited by anything, least of all by our insufficiencies. He is the great I Am. He is all we could ever want or need, and then some. He can do things before we think we're ready for them. He blesses us even when we don't deserve to be blessed. Our weaknesses don't slow him down; they only highlight his strength.

He's that good. He's that great. We'll spend the rest of our lives being continually overwhelmed by his goodness and his grace.

What circumstances are you facing that need the life of God? What dreams and hopes have died and become entombed? Jesus wants to roll the stone away. For Lazarus, he was the source of resurrection and life. For Moses, he was the source of security and deliverance. God is your source, your sufficiency, your salvation.

Maybe you've concluded that God will not help you until you get all your ducks in a row and fix all your faults and solve all your failures and weaknesses. Let me remind you that we serve a God who is the same yesterday, today, and forever.

He can save you all by himself. He can help you even if—especially if—you don't deserve it, earn it, predict it, prepare for it, or even believe it. He is a today God. He is a now God. And he is here for you.

6

Pillow Talk

Flat and Fluffy

Possibly my least favorite verse in the Bible is found in the book of Proverbs, chapter 20. Verse 13 says, "Do not love sleep, lest you come to poverty; open your eyes, and you will be satisfied with bread."

I understand that verse and I agree with that verse. My problem is that I really enjoy sleep. I don't love it, though—that would be unbiblical. I just like it. A lot.

Thankfully, that isn't all the Bible has to say about sleep. Proverbs, chapter 3, verse 24 says, "When you lie down, you will not be afraid; yes, you will lie down and your sleep will be sweet."

For parents of small children, that verse is a little taste of heaven. God could have made this universe so there would always be sunlight, and he could have created us without the need for sleep or rest. But he had pity. He was merciful and gracious toward parents of small children, because he knew that those children needed to be neutralized and tranquilized and silenced for a few hours, for the sanity of their parents.

I realize how much I appreciate the gift of sleep when my sleep is interrupted. This is usually done by one of my three offspring. Yes, I realize I should be compassionate that they suddenly and desperately and immediately need a drink of water. I know I should be happy to answer their random life questions that came to them in a dream. I know that all too soon they will grow up and be gone. But I really, really like my sleep.

I know what my wife is going to think when she reads this. Out of the deep crevices and bitterness of her heart, she is going to say, "What? Are you kidding me? You never wake up with our offspring. I am always the one. You just cover your ears with a pillow and sleep soundly." And that's true. She usually, sometimes, most of the time, always gets up with our children.

There is something incredibly refreshing about digging into your favorite pillow and going to a very happy place.

I have a pillow structure, personally. I have a flat pillow and a fluffy pillow. I call them Flat and Fluffy. Sometimes I stack Flat on Fluffy, and sometimes I stack Fluffy on Flat. It's totally my prerogative.

When I'm traveling, I miss Flat and Fluffy. When I'm in a hotel, and my wife is not there, I miss her—but I miss Flat and Fluffy too. They are the one-two punch of blessing in my life. Flat and Fluffy are there when I need them most.

Actually, one of the most powerful descriptions of Jesus in the Bible involves a pillow. The context of the story is what makes it so powerful: Jesus was sound asleep on a pillow, in a boat, on a lake, during the storm of the century.

Apparently this experience made a big impact on the disciples because Matthew, Mark, and Luke all recount the story. Chapter 4, verses 35–41, of the Gospel of Mark says,

> When evening had come, He said to them, "Let us cross over to the other side." Now when they had left the multitude, they took Him along in the boat as He was. And other little boats were also with Him. And a great windstorm arose, and the waves beat into the boat, so that it was already filling. But He was in the stern, asleep on a pillow. And they awoke Him and said to Him, "Teacher, do You not care that we are perishing?"
>
> Then He arose and rebuked the wind, and said to the sea, "Peace, be still!" And the wind ceased and there was a great calm. But He said to them, "Why are you so fearful? How is it that you have no faith?"
>
> And they feared exceedingly, and said to one another, "Who can this be, that even the wind and the sea obey Him!"

Jesus and his disciples set sail on what was supposed to be a short trip across the lake, sort of a *Gilligan's Island* three-hour tour, if you will. But a serious storm comes up, and the disciples are terrified.

Keep in mind that these guys are professional fishermen.

They are used to being on the water day or night, in all kinds of conditions. They aren't newbies, they aren't hobbyists, and they aren't tourists looking for some fun in the sun.

These young men had probably grown up on this body of water. They've probably seen the good, the bad, and the ugly. And yet, at this moment, they fear for their lives. It is quite possibly a storm unlike any they had ever seen. They are frantic.

Meanwhile, at the back of the boat, Jesus has his divine head on a pillow, and he's asleep. The disciples are screaming at a pitch that's only appropriate for junior high girls, and Jesus is snoring.

The contrast is massive, and it's intentional. I think Jesus is preaching us a message from his place of rest. He is telling us that when the storms of life come, we can trust him. We can look at his attitude of peace and find rest for our souls.

Soaked but Not Sunk

Before we continue talking about Jesus and his pillow, let me make a couple of points. First, just because Jesus is in the boat doesn't mean we won't go through storms.

Storms happen.

Bumper stickers say that differently, but I'm going to keep it G-rated here. Stuff happens, storms happen, troubles happen. Bad things happen to good people, to people who follow God and love God and believe in God.

Storms don't mean Jesus is not in our lives. Storms are no indication of our lack of faith or lack of holiness. I've heard people say things like, "Oh, you're in a storm? You're facing trouble? You must have done something wrong, or you must not have enough faith that God can rescue you."

But that's not what the Bible teaches. The Bible teaches that we all face storms. But Jesus is in our boat, and he's not freaking out. Maybe we should take a hint.

Second, just because we have Jesus in our boat doesn't mean we won't get wet. That is, just because we love and follow Jesus doesn't mean we won't be affected by the circumstances of life.

Maybe some of us are in a storm right now, and we aren't just wet—we are soaked. Maybe we are drenched and embarrassed and ashamed, because we think we should be stronger or we should be smarter. We think that because Jesus is in our lives, we should always be happy and victorious and unaffected. We worry that if anyone finds out how the elements and circumstances are getting to us, they are going to reject us. So in the name of faith, we fake a smile and act like we're dry.

But there's a difference between soaked and sunk. We might be drenched, but we are not drowned. We might be wet, but our heads are above water. We might be damaged and discouraged and distracted by the craziness of life, but we know who is in our boat. We're not going down.

It's not hypocrisy to love God and thank God when you're wet. Jesus isn't bothered by how wet we are. He's happy to help us get past the storms and arrive safely at the other side.

God is on our side no matter what kind of storm we face, and he's on our side no matter who caused the storm. God is with us even when we created the storm ourselves, maybe through bad choices or unwise actions.

The storm is not the point. The wind and waves and water are not the point. Jesus is the point. No matter what you are going through or why you are going through it, Jesus is calm and in control.

Keep Calm and Sail On

That said, I doubt the disciples are thinking along such lines at this point in the story. No, they are paddling for their lives.

And they are getting more and more frustrated every time they look back and see their leader asleep. This is the guy responsible for getting them into this, and he doesn't seem to care. How many times do they glare at him before finally someone decides to wake him up?

I think they expect him to leap up, scream a little, grab an oar, and paddle furiously for shore. That's what they want, actually. They want him to lead the paddling and the panic.

Sometimes, when life is crazy, I find myself expecting God to panic alongside me. I think he should be just as nervous as I am, that he should be sitting on the edge of his throne or pacing heaven's hallways, waiting to see what the outcome of my storm will be.

But God seems to be asleep. It's frustrating. Doesn't God know that my circumstances are about to overwhelm me? Can't he see that I am soaked and sinking? Why doesn't he do something?

Finally, the disciples wake Jesus up. He probably takes his time sitting up. He yawns and stretches. He rubs his eyes. He's really drawing out the suspense. Then he turns toward the storm.

"Wind, waves—stop it."

The sea turns to glass. The wind evaporates. In the distance, seagulls are faintly cawing or crying or making whatever sounds seagulls make.

I think there is a pregnant pause. Maybe Peter lets loose a few expletives. He's a fisherman, after all.

The disciples look at Jesus and their jaws drop to the deck. "Who is this man? Who talks to storms—and they obey him? Who does that?"

The Bible uses words like *feared exceedingly, marveled,* and *afraid* to describe their reaction. That doesn't mean they are afraid of Jesus like they had been afraid of the storm. It means they are deeply in awe of him. They are astonished and stunned and dumbfounded and awestruck.

I think right about now they realize that in reality, they were never in danger of dying. God can't sink. He isn't going to accidentally drown in the water he created in the first place. Winds and waves and storms are nothing in comparison to the man who was asleep in their boat.

Awe and Wonder

It's easy to be in awe of Jesus after the storm. But the point of this passage is that we should be in awe of Jesus during the storm.

At the end of the story the disciples ask in wonder, "Who can this be, that even the wind and the sea obey Him?"

You know what they should have said? They should have looked at Jesus, sleeping soundly on Flat and Fluffy, and said, "Who can this be, that even the wind and the sea cannot wake him?" They should have looked at Jesus' calm demeanor and realized that he had everything under control even when the storm was raging.

The word *awe* refers to an overwhelming sense of wonder and admiration produced by something powerful. When we are in awe of something, we revere and fear it.

In life, it's almost as if storms seek to sway us and to steal our awe. They want to garner our reverence, and they attempt to convince us of their power.

That was the problem with these young disciples. They were in awe of the storm even when Jesus was so near. They looked at the elements. They listened to their five senses rather than trusting Jesus.

Our five senses shout at us when we are in the challenges and difficulties of life. We can hear the storm. We can see the storm. We can smell the storm and feel the storm. Our senses tell us, "You're going down! You'll never last! What will you do now?"

I'm not advocating that we ignore reality; rather, we should pay attention to a greater reality. Jesus is with us, and he is unfazed by the circumstances that so easily rock our boats and our world. He is in the storm with us. He will neither leave nor forsake us. His promises are true and his love never fails.

Note what the disciples said to Jesus when they woke him up: "Don't you care that we are dying here?" They criticize him because he refuses to fret and worry and panic along with them.

When we are in awe of Jesus rather than the storm, we will find ourselves facing the same criticism. Coworkers and friends will accuse us: "You don't even care. Don't you see the economy? Don't you see the sickness? Don't you see the potential for destruction or loss or death? You should care more!"

And by "care more," of course, they mean bite your nails more, pace more, stress out more, sweat more, and complain more. That's how most people are used to functioning. If you aren't visibly worried, they think you're either dumb or indifferent.

God disagrees.

The Bible says in Matthew, chapter 6, that if you're short and you worry about it, you won't get any taller. If you're balding and you stress out about it, you aren't going to grow any more hair. In the same way, if your business is short on funds, worry isn't going to help you make payroll. If your kids are going crazy, worry won't help them make good choices.

Worry is useless. Worry saps our strength and steals our focus. It causes us to be more awestruck and dumbfounded by storms than by the one who silences storms with a word.

A few years ago, my family went through a storm of illness

that we could never have imagined. Out of the blue, my father was diagnosed with incurable cancer.

For six years, my dad fought with courage, faith, and grace. Ultimately, he graduated from this life. He is healed now, in heaven. He is healthy, whole, and happy. One day I will see him again, and we will swap stories about the crazy ups and downs of life, and about how good God is, and about how we used to cheat at golf. He meant the world to me and I will love him forever.

The storm of cancer assailed my family beyond anything we had ever experienced. We were buffeted by the winds and soaked by the waves. Many times I stood by my dad's bedside as he experienced aches and pains. I watched and hurt as his body grew weaker.

In those moments, cancer wanted my awe. It wanted my reverence and wonder and admiration. "Look how strong I am," it would say. "Look what I can do."

There was only one way to resist the pull of cancer's power. It was to look at Jesus. I couldn't out-argue cancer. I couldn't outwit the circumstances. I couldn't calm the storm.

But I could look to Jesus. He was with us through the good times and the bad. He was there when the suffering seemed too hard to bear. He was there when the circumstances didn't make sense, when the choices were too hard to make, and when our senses were screaming that all was lost.

Jesus never let us sink.

Cancer, bankruptcy, AIDS, divorce, depression, rape, suicide—these are storms so powerful that there can seem to be no hope of tomorrow. But they are not more powerful than Jesus. They are not more wonderful or sublime than God.

Through it all, Jesus is asking us to look at him and to focus on him. He is nearby. He is in our boat, and he is at peace and at rest because he is greater than the storm.

"Son, you're not going down. Daughter, I know your senses are screaming at you, but keep your eyes on me. We're going to get to the other side."

Storms happen. I can't promise that you won't get wet. I can't promise that you won't go through tough times. But I can promise that Jesus is bigger than your storm and that he is with you. The storm will end. The wind will cease. The waves will be still. Jesus will see you safely through to the other side.

7

Trust Grace

I'll Forgive You—Tomorrow

I was raised in a family that believed in conflict resolution. My dad loved to quote Ephesians, chapter 4, verse 26: "Do not let the sun go down on your wrath." That was the rule. You could duke it out for a bit, but before you went to bed, you had to have resolution and forgiveness.

My dad and mom made my sister and me kiss on the cheek at the end of every one of our fights. It was brilliant, actually. We stopped fighting because kissing each other was worse than any punishment. I grew up with the mentality that reconciliation and forgiveness should be a normal part of family life.

Now I have a marriage and family of my own. Chelsea and I have been married for fourteen years and counting. We have a great marriage, and we love each other deeply.

We have an ongoing contest in our marriage. It's an

unspoken contest, but it's very real. Anytime we have a fight—which obviously only happens like once a day—we have a contest to see who will say this first: "Will you forgive me?"

In this little contest between Chelsea and me, the idea is that the most spiritual person in the marriage will be the first to say, "Will you forgive me?"

That sounds great, and in theory I'm totally for it. It's just that Chelsea always wins, because she's spiritual and smart and disciplined. I am spiritual, too, I think—but I'm also emotional. Really emotional. It's not a fair contest.

So we will be at the pinnacle of our skirmish, right at the zenith of our fight. And my veins are bulging and I'm starting to spit a little when I talk.

And that's when she'll say, "Will you forgive me?"

I'm not ready for that. I'm like, "Whoa! Too soon."

She's sincere. "Really, babe, I'm sorry. Will you forgive me?"

And inside I'm thinking: *No. I mean, yes—but tomorrow. Right now, I have some really good points to make, and I want you to feel bad because you made me feel bad. Actually I want you to wallow in regret and remorse and to experience the agony you inflicted upon me. I will forgive you later. Right now, I want justice.*

Do you know what I'm talking about? Most of us have been there. We don't actually say all those things, of course, but the emotions are there and they are real.

This is not fair. You can't just get out of this by asking me to forgive you. I'm not finished making you suffer. You need to earn my forgiveness. You need to beg for it.

Chelsea does it right when I'm most upset. And I'm like, "F-f-f-fine. I forgive you. I don't want to, but I will."

She's right, of course. People in healthy relationships are quick to forgive, quick to forget, and quick to move on.

But I know I'm not alone in my desire to be vindicated or to air my side of the grievance. It's human nature to want justice, at least when it's to our benefit. When we are in the wrong, we are all about grace; but when the other person is wrong, justice seems so godly and biblical and divine.

Eleventh-Hour Justice

If we are going to trust God and enjoy God and love life, we have to understand how God views justice and relationships.

We tend to base our relationships on justice and fairness because we feel a measure of control. We know what to do, we know what to expect, and we know what we deserve. But Jesus has a habit of messing with our concept of justice. Matthew chapter 20 gives us a parable told by Jesus that does just that. I'm going to start with the last verse of chapter 19.

> But many who are first will be last, and the last first. For the kingdom of heaven is like a landowner who went out early in the morning to hire laborers for his vineyard. Now when he had agreed with the laborers for a denarius a day, he sent them into his vineyard. And he went out about the third hour and saw others standing idle in the marketplace, and

said to them, "You also go into the vineyard, and whatever is right I will give you." So they went. Again he went out about the sixth and the ninth hour, and did likewise. And about the eleventh hour he went out and found others standing idle, and said to them, "Why have you been standing here idle all day?"

They said to him, "Because no one hired us."

He said to them, "You also go into the vineyard, and whatever is right you will receive."

So when evening had come, the owner of the vineyard said to his steward, "Call the laborers and give them their wages, beginning with the last to the first." And when those came who were hired about the eleventh hour, they each received a denarius. But when the first came, they supposed that they would receive more; and they likewise received each a denarius.

And when they had received it, they complained against the landowner, saying, "These last men have worked only one hour, and you made them equal to us who have borne the burden and the heat of the day."

But he answered one of them and said, "Friend, I am doing you no wrong. Did you not agree with me for a denarius? Take what is yours and go your way. I wish to give to this last man the same as to you. Is it not lawful for me to do what I wish with my own things? Or is your eye evil because I am good?"

So the last will be first, and the first last. For many are called, but few chosen.

Jesus starts this parable by saying that this is what his kingdom is like: the last are first and the first are last. In other words, in the domain, culture, and community that Jesus is building, our ranking systems are backward. Jesus is redefining our idea of justice.

Why is this important? Because if we try to relate to God based on what we've done, what we deserve, and what we think he should do for us, we're going to end up as confused as these vineyard workers.

God's idea of justice requires a great deal of trust from us. We have to believe he is good and he will take care of us.

As human beings we naturally think along the lines of what we've earned and what we deserve and what is fair. But Jesus says, "Let me tell you what my kingdom is like" and proceeds to tell a story that is flat-out frustrating. It's frustrating unless you're the eleventh-hour worker, that is.

I find that often when I'm disturbed or discouraged, it isn't because my life is terrible. It's because something in my life isn't meeting my expectations. God isn't doing what I think he should, and I have a hard time just letting go and trusting him. I've noticed that how much I enjoy God and life is directly tied to how much I trust God in my life.

Just like this ancient culture, we have a ranking system. It usually exists in the secrecy and the crevices of our hearts, but we all classify each other. We all rank each other.

"Wow, that's a beautiful person, a real top-shelf kind of beauty."

"That woman is such an excellent human being."

"He's a gifted guy. Amazing talent."

"Um, him—not so talented. Not so gifted."

"Whoa . . . hard to look at."

You know what I mean? We all have our class system.

Jesus essentially says, "I understand how you think. I understand you have first place and second place and eighth place and dead last. You have a ranking system, but you need to understand my ranking system. Many whom you think are first are actually going to be last; and many whom you think are last are actually going to be first."

"Uh, wait. What?"

Notice in Jesus' parable that the only group of workers with a contract with the landowner is the first group. They agree to work a full day—twelve hours—for one denarius, which was a standard day's wage. This is a fair agreement. They work an honest day and they get paid an honest day's wages. Everyone knows what to expect. Everyone is happy with the terms.

At the third hour, which would have been around nine o'clock, the landowner goes back and hires some more workers. These workers, however, are hired on trust, not on contract. The owner doesn't tell them how much he is going to pay them. He just says, "I'll pay you whatever is right."

He does the same thing at the sixth hour and ninth hour, or noon and three o'clock. Finally, at the eleventh hour, an hour before quitting time, he hires one last group. And he tells them the same thing: "Trust me. I'll pay you what is right. I'll pay you fairly."

Then the work is done, the whistle blows, and it's time to get paid. This is where the friction starts.

It's fascinating to me that the landowner insists that his paymaster pay first the guys who arrived last. Why didn't he pay the first workers first? That would have made sense. Or maybe pay them in alphabetical order? Or have them line up randomly? The landowner seems a bit sadistic, like he's trying to pick a fight here.

Actually Jesus is making a point: grace can be frustrating.

"Okay, eleventh-hour guys. Where are you?" The paymaster has his bag of coins in hand. So the workers who showed up an hour before quitting come forward. They are fresh and energetic and they smell nice. They never broke a sweat. Their manicures are impeccable.

The owner says, "We agreed that I would pay you what is fair, right? So here's a denarius for you, and a denarius for you, and one for you . . ."

The guys who have been working for twelve hours are way at the end of the line, but they are really paying attention. They've been wondering how this was going to go down. Instantly they start doing the math. "They got a denarius? That's crazy. Guaranteed we must be getting a lot more than that. Awesome."

The paymaster goes through the next three groups of workers. "Denarius, denarius, denarius."

Finally he gets to the guys who were there first, the guys who were under contract. "A denarius for you, and one for you . . ."

"What? Hey! No fair!"

"I'm sorry. Is there a problem?"

"Yes, actually, now that you mention it. We bore the heat of the day. It's like Phoenix, Arizona, out here. These guys worked at twilight. They still smell nice."

The early group was keeping track, weren't they? Why weren't they just busy working? Instead, they're like, "They worked one hour. We counted. We clocked them. One hour. And you're going to give them the same as us? Haven't we earned more? Where's the justice in all of this?"

What is Jesus saying? That God doesn't give us what we think we deserve. He gives us what he wants to give us, and he asks us to trust him that it is right.

Some of us read this and think, *Actually, I'd rather have justice. I understand justice. Justice is quantifiable and predictable and comfortable. I want to deserve what I get, and I want to get what I deserve.*

Really—we want to come into contract with God? We want to talk about what we deserve? That's a dead end. We don't want to go there. The Bible says in Romans 6:23 that the wages of sin is death. If we're going to get technical about it, that's what we deserve. Anything more is sheer grace and mercy.

So let's stop talking in terms of what we deserve, and what we've earned, and what is just. If that really plays out, you and I are doomed. We are all products of grace. We are all saved by grace. Let's remember that and celebrate that.

You know what's amazing? Had the first group been paid first, they wouldn't have known how much the last workers received. Sometimes I wonder how happy you and I would be if we didn't have information about our neighbors and our friends.

I'm convinced God blesses people in front of us on purpose. You were so happy that God gave you a cat, but then you find out he gave Bill an SUV, and now you're mad. You were excited about your little Siamese, but now Bill gets an Escalade and you're frustrated.

"Come on, God. I get a house cat and Bill gets an Escalade?" If you didn't know that Bill got an Escalade, you'd still be happy with the cat. But now you're like, "I want an Escalade, like Bill."

At the end of the book of John, Jesus singled out Peter and encouraged him. If you remember, Peter needed some love—recently he had failed spectacularly in his commitment to be faithful to Jesus. Jesus told Peter that he was important, that he would be a leader, and that he would be so faithful to Jesus that one day he would indeed die for him.

Then Peter turned around and saw John, and he said, "Hey, Jesus, what about John? What's he going to get?"

And Jesus essentially said to Peter, "What's John got to do with you? This isn't about John and me, this is about you and me. What are you asking about John for? If I want John to live forever, what does that have to do with you?"

Jesus was making an exaggerated statement to prove a point: "I'll do whatever I want between John and me. This is about you and me. Just follow me."

In other words, just work in the vineyard. Quit comparing. Quit complaining. Quit overthinking it.

"God, I've served you faithfully for so many years, but I can barely pay my bills. Meanwhile this guy over here who's made a mess of his life, he starts following you and suddenly he gets a better job and higher income than me. I'm frustrated. I'm aggravated. Where is the justice?"

No wonder we don't enjoy God sometimes. We're too busy second-guessing him.

Whatever Is Right

The first group of laborers in the parable was under contract, but the last four groups were under grace. They were living and serving based on trust. *Whatever is right.* How cool is that? God's idea of what is right is far more generous than ours. His concept of justice and fairness blows our petty little measures out of the water.

I would much rather live in the ambiguity of God's grace and goodness than in the strict measures of legalism and law.

It comes down to this: Do we trust God? Do we trust that whatever he deems right will be enough? Do we trust that he is just, that he is right, that he is good, and that he is merciful?

Let's enjoy his goodness. Let's enjoy his grace. There is so much freedom in just letting God be God, in maintaining a childlike innocence and faith in him.

Just in case you were wondering who the eleventh-hour people are, that would be you and me. We barely got in. When we met God, our lives were going nowhere.

God said, "What are you doing here?"

We replied, "We don't really know. We're just here."

And God said, "I'll take you. You'll be mine. You follow me, and I'll give you whatever is right."

I'm planning to spend the rest of my life just happy that God loves me, that he has forgiven me, and that he has made me his own. Is that too simplistic? I'm happy. God is good. I have so much to be grateful for.

When we've been on a good run—you know, when we've been nice to people, and we haven't sinned very much, and we're reading our Bibles and even highlighting some parts—it's tempting to start thinking in terms of what we deserve.

Do not give in to that temptation. What we deserve is so much less than what he wants to give us. Why insist on what we deserve?

Working in God's field, by the way, is not meant to be a metaphor for how hard it is to follow God. Jesus is actually saying the opposite: that following God is about his generosity and grace, not about what we do or don't do. It is a joy to follow God. It is rewarding to obey him. His goodness toward us is far beyond anything we could earn or deserve.

We relate to God according to his rich measures of grace and generosity. We don't have to worry about whether we measure up or whether we are working hard enough to please him. We don't have to stress out about the future. We don't have to waste our energy envying other people. We can simply enjoy God and trust God and love God.

By the way, this will completely change the way we relate to others. It will make for great friendships. When we trust

God to give us what is right, we can celebrate the good things God does for other people. That's where we really begin to enjoy life. Instead of complaining that you got a cat and Bill got an Escalade, take your cat over for a ride in Bill's Escalade.

Ephesians, chapter 3, says, "Now to Him who is able to do exceedingly abundantly above all that we ask or think, according to the power that works in us, to Him be glory in the church by Christ Jesus to all generations, forever and ever" (verses 20–21). There are more superlatives packed in here than any passage has a right to have.

I want to follow a God who blesses me beyond what I could dream up. He knows me better than I know myself. He loves me more than I love myself. He sees every detail of my past, present, and future, and he is taking care of me.

I am not going to relate to God based on a contract. I'm not going to relate to him based on what I deserve or earn. I'm just going to let him surprise me out of his infinite goodness and grace and mercy. And I know that I will receive exceedingly abundantly above all that I can ask, think, or even imagine.

This is a relationship. This is a friendship. Let's not reduce it to a legal agreement. Let's stay free and trusting and happy.

8

A Passerby

How to Look Awesome

I love carbs, something we talked about in chapter 4. Bread, pastries, pasta, chips—these are awesome foods. The great thing about carbs is that they work at any time. If you're feeling down, carbs can pick you up. If you're feeling awesome, carbs are a great way to celebrate. It doesn't matter what time of day it is. Breakfast, lunch, dinner, or late-night snack, carbs are always the perfect fit.

I know fitness gurus and doctors tell us to be careful with carbs. I don't want to. I want to be reckless with carbs. Unfortunately, my total obsession with carbs is equal to my total disinterest in working out. So I'm constantly living in the tension of hating working out and loving carbs.

I've noticed that before I work out, I'm always moaning and groaning and bemoaning the thought of exerting myself. By the way, when I say "work out," I'm referencing thirty minutes on a treadmill. At a brisk walk. On an incline. Are you impressed? That is my idea of strenuous physical exercise.

But when I consider working out, my first reaction is, "Oh, I don't know. I'm tired. It's Monday. Monday is after Sunday. I preached six times yesterday, and I want to take a breather."

Then Tuesday comes. I'm like, "Chelsea, we have staff meeting today, and I've got some other appointments and meetings. I've got to conserve my energy."

Wednesday is always a travel day, because I preach at our LA campus that night. So I can't exercise on Wednesday.

Thursday? Well, Thursday is after Wednesday, and I need a break because I preached twice the night before.

Friday is family day. It's all about the kids. Working out would be selfish.

Saturday? That's prep day for Sunday.

As you can see, I have a great excuse to never work out for the rest of my life. This is awesome.

But when I actually hit the treadmill and walk half an hour at 3.5 mph, I get pumped. I feel great. The endorphins kick in, and I'm like, "Man, I feel awesome! I'm going to do this every day."

You know the guy who wants everyone to know he worked out? That would be me. I am that guy. I mean, why else would I be working out?

A trainer asked me once, "What are your goals?"

I said, "To look awesome! I wouldn't be here if eating ice cream made me look awesome. I want to look like Wolverine."

He was like, "What about health?"

"I think Wolverine is pretty healthy. That's how I see it."

I tweeted the other day after being at the gym: "I worked out." Really? Who does that? Then I came home and flexed for my kids, and I asked my son, "Zion, you want some of this?"

He was like, "It's so hairy, Dad; it's so hairy."

I love working out—after I'm done. But before I do it, I hate it; and while I'm doing it, I hate it even more. Why does it work this way?

Now when it comes to carbs, it's the complete opposite. Before I eat carbs, I love them. And while I'm eating them, I love them even more. But when I'm done? Regret and remorse move in instantly. "Oh, I shouldn't have eaten at this restaurant. I hate this place. I hate my life. I feel bloated."

Sometimes I pray, "God, why did you have to make it like this? Everything that tastes awesome makes you look huge. And everything that tastes horrible makes you look awesome. Why, God, why?"

I don't understand it.

Take Up Your Cross

The point of my confession and rant is that life is paradoxical. Often what we really want doesn't materialize until we do what we really don't want to do.

This brings us again to Mark, chapter 8, verses 34–37. We read this earlier, when we talked about what it means to deny yourself. Now I want to look at what it means to take up your cross.

Whoever desires to come after Me, let him deny himself, and take up his cross, and follow Me. For whoever desires to save his life will lose it, but whoever loses his life for My sake and the gospel's will save it. For what will it profit a man if he gains the whole world, and loses his own soul? Or what will a man give in exchange for his soul?

Jesus is giving us an invitation to life. The invitation is to truly live: not just to exist, not just to breathe, but to live life as it was meant to be lived. But his invitation to this existence is paradoxical. God's invitation to life comes through death.

Taking up your cross is a dramatic image. Today, we tend to look at crosses as nice, sweet religious symbols. That is not how ancient Israel or any other nation that the Romans had conquered viewed crosses. The Romans used crosses to publicly execute criminals and dissenters. They were torture instruments. They meant humiliation, pain, suffering, and death. So when Jesus said, "Take up your cross," people had an instant mental image. And it wasn't exactly a cheerful one.

We often have the same reaction. Sometimes we think Jesus is telling us that following him means humiliation, pain, and suffering. It means we won't be happy and we will never eat carbs. *This life is all about suffering,* some people think, *but at least we'll be happy in heaven.*

That's not very motivating. Does following Jesus mean nothing but crosses and losses?

Don't get me wrong. I know life has hard moments, and I know following Jesus is not always easy. I'm not promising anyone a pain-free or trouble-free life if they follow Jesus. But I don't think Jesus is saying life in his service is always going to be horrible. He actually gives us an invitation to abundant life, both here on this planet and for eternity.

We access that abundant life by giving up control. The point of this passage is not what we do for Jesus: it's what he does for us when we trust him completely. In other words, this isn't so much about our heroic self-denial as it is about Jesus leading us into life. He is the hero here, not us. We follow him because he is the source of life.

When you look at it that way, it's hard to call it sacrifice. Following Jesus is the best decision we could make.

It's interesting that Jesus doesn't say *my* cross; he says *your* cross. It is our cross because we deserve it. According to the Bible, we've sinned, and the penalty for sin is death.

It's even more interesting that Jesus doesn't say *die* on your cross; he says *take* or carry your cross. We don't die on our crosses, at least not in the sense of paying for our sin, because Jesus died on his cross instead of us.

When we carry our crosses—when we choose to trust and follow Jesus—we gain the benefits of his cross. He carried his cross and died on it so I could be truly free.

Jesus is encouraging us to identify with his death and resurrection because that is the source of abundant, satisfying life. He is calling us to stop focusing on self and instead focus on him. He is asking us to lose our lives in the sense that we become so wrapped up in him that we no longer think about our wants and desires.

Jim Elliot, a Christian missionary who ended up giving his life for the gospel in the Amazon jungle, said this: "He is no fool who gives what he cannot keep to gain what he cannot lose."* When we understand that Jesus is the source of life, it isn't hard to trust him or follow him or even die for him.

Death Walk

For the people listening to Jesus, *take up your cross* would have brought to mind a Roman custom often called the death walk. The death walk was when a criminal condemned to die by crucifixion was made to pick up his cross and carry it to his place of execution. The road would be lined with a gallery of people, because crucifixions were a public spectacle.

The condemned criminal would shoulder the wooden beam and carry it down this road of ridicule, and jeering crowds would spit on him and throw things at him and mock him.

If the criminal was physically unable to carry the cross because of the torture he had already received, Roman officers leading the execution would sometimes compel an innocent bystander to carry the cross.

Jesus himself did not carry his own cross. His cross was carried by an innocent man, a passerby who was randomly and inconveniently compelled to carry Jesus' cross. His name was Simon.

---

*   Jim Elliot, quoted in Elisabeth Elliot, *Shadow of the Almighty* (New York: Harper, 1958), 15.

I think every detail in the Bible is there on purpose. In this story, Simon's intersection with Jesus' death walk is a beautiful picture of taking up our cross. Mark describes the scene in chapter 15:

> And when they had mocked Him, they took the purple off Him, put His own clothes on Him, and led Him out to crucify Him. Then they compelled a certain man, Simon a Cyrenian, the father of Alexander and Rufus, as he was coming out of the country and passing by, to bear His cross. And they brought Him to the place called Golgotha. (verses 20–22)

We don't know a lot about Simon. This incident, which is recorded in three of the four gospels, is his claim to fame in the Bible. But there are enough details to begin to put ourselves in the story.

We do know Simon is from Cyrene, in northern Africa. He is likely in town both for the Passover and for business. When the story starts, he is on his way in from the country. He probably plans to conclude his business, celebrate the festival, and return home. Simon's schedule does not include stopping to watch the crucifixion of Jesus. He is a passerby.

Suddenly he hears a shout.

"You! Come here! Carry this cross," a Roman officer says to Simon.

What? Me? Simon thinks. *Are you serious? I don't have time for this.*

"Yes sir," he replies. He has no choice. He doesn't dare disobey a Roman officer.

Simon is probably thinking, *Are you kidding me? Talk about an inconvenience! Who is this mangled and beaten man? Clearly he's done something wrong. He deserves this. He's hated and he's despised.*

The Roman soldiers hoist the cross onto Simon's shoulder. He is carrying this rough, heavy symbol of crime and death, thinking, *I don't have time for this.*

He walks between a gallery of people who are spitting and cursing and ridiculing Jesus. I know what I'd be thinking if I were in his place. *Hey, I don't even know this guy. Don't spit on me. Don't throw things at me. I'm just a businessman. I'm just in town from Africa. I don't deserve to carry a cross. I'm innocent.*

Simon doesn't realize that this interruption, this bother, will turn out to be one of the highest privileges in human history. He is just a passerby, but he has the honor of being the man who carried the cross of the Savior of the world. What he thinks is a nuisance becomes part of the story that changed history.

We like our schedules, don't we? And schedules are important. We have to plan, we have to budget, and we have to prepare. But God's interruptions are often the most meaningful moments in our lives.

I think part of the spirit and the heart behind Jesus' call to pick up our cross is that we would learn to trust him with our schedules, that we would trust him with our plans and priorities and goals.

We can get so obsessed with the funny little plans that we make. We need to learn to welcome God's interruptions, because his interruptions and inconveniences are the portals to truly living.

Proverbs 16:9 says, "A man's heart plans his way, but the LORD directs his steps." It is wise and good and prudent to make plans, but we have to keep in mind that our lives are part of a bigger picture. Simon had no idea of the magnitude of what was taking place in front of him. He had no idea that his unexpected and unscheduled stop would play a part in the salvation of mankind. From his perspective, it was a nuisance. From history's perspective, it was his greatest achievement.

The Bible doesn't record what happened to Simon after this incident. Interestingly, this passage does mention his two children, Rufus and Alexander. Why? Some scholars think that these two young men were well-known figures in the Christian community that Mark was writing to.

If so, then this might well have been a defining moment in their spiritual journeys. It is likely that Simon and his sons ultimately recognized that the man who randomly interrupted their schedules was the Savior of mankind.

Imagine the stories Simon could tell to his kids, his grand-kids, and his great-grandkids. "I was there, you know? I walked with him and I watched him."

"Really, Grandpa? What was it like?"

"At first, I didn't realize who he was. I was just minding my own business when suddenly Jesus was standing in front of me. He looked at me. He said my name. I've never seen love in anyone's eyes like that. He was on his way to die for me, and I got to help carry the cross. What an honor and privilege! That day—it changed my life forever."

God is at work helping humanity. He included Simon in the story, and he wants to include you and me as well. We are privileged to be part of something far bigger than ourselves.

Sure, we have schedules and jobs; but in all of this, let's let Jesus be the most important. Let's trust him to lead. The interruptions and inconveniences in our days might be more significant than we realize.

Jesus is the object of our obsession. We are preoccupied with him. We can follow him anywhere and everywhere. We can trust him implicitly.

God is real, and he wants you to find life. How? By losing yourself in his beauty. By losing yourself in the grandeur of the good news of what he's done on your behalf. When we find ourselves in this space, we discover what it means to truly live.

LIFE IS to be at peace with God and yourself.

I don't think I exaggerate when I say that peace is one of the deepest and most basic human needs. We search for peace in our emotions, peace in our minds, peace in our circumstances, and peace in our relationships. We long for stability and constancy in a world often characterized by chaos.

Although our culture seems to specialize in distraction and hectic schedules, the search for peace has been around for a long, long time. That's why Jesus had a lot to say about it.

Jesus lived a real life with real people who had real needs. These people had the same personality quirks and temptations and pressures we experience today. Sure, they didn't use terms like OCD or ADHD, and they wore robes instead of skinny jeans, and they never dreamed of indoor plumbing or paying four bucks for a cup of coffee— but they were people like you and me.

So when Jesus taught, his words weren't just pleasant

spiritual platitudes. They were real-time responses to the needs of humanity. They were life and they were wisdom. In our complex and often confusing culture, Jesus' path to peace resonates more than ever.

9

Many Things

The Many-Things Syndrome

One of my favorite snapshots of Jesus explaining how to truly be at peace is found in the book of Luke, chapter 10. The setting is the house of Mary, Martha, and Lazarus, whom I mentioned earlier. These three siblings were some of Jesus' closest friends during his years here on earth.

In the story, we find Mary and Martha engaging in a bit of sibling rivalry.

> Now it happened as they went that He entered a certain village; and a certain woman named Martha welcomed Him into her house. And she had a sister called Mary, who also sat at Jesus' feet and heard His word. But Martha was distracted with much serving, and she approached Him and said, "Lord, do You not care that my sister has left me to serve alone? Therefore tell her to help me."

And Jesus answered and said to her, "Martha, Martha, you are worried and troubled about many things. But one thing is needed, and Mary has chosen that good part, which will not be taken away from her." (verses 38–42)

I don't know about you, but I can relate to Martha. Not that I am good at cooking or household chores—I can relate to Martha in her distraction. Maybe you can too. Martha is like most of us: we are awesome at being busy and staying stressed and operating on overload.

My phone certainly does not help this condition, as I confessed earlier. I can wake up, pick up my phone, and check my iMessages, text messages, voice mail, e-mail, Twitter, Instagram, Facebook, Vine, Pinterest, YouTube, Snapchat, Skype, Google Plus, and maybe even MySpace. And say hi to Siri. I can do all of this before engaging with physically present human beings.

We all face distractions. Life comes fast and furious. New technology, new forms of communication, and social media have heightened the level at which we live and think and communicate.

I have friends who are almost insulted if I do not respond to their text message within the proper five-minute window. That's the expectancy now. They're like, "You took seven minutes to respond to my text. Are we still friends?"

I'm not against technology. I'm not against big-city living. I'm not against hobbies, or having fun, or Facebook, or any of those things. But our lifestyle and our culture can easily lead us into a state of mind that I call the Many-Things Syndrome.

Jesus told Martha she was worried and troubled about *many things*, but that somehow Mary had discovered the *one thing* that was needed. Martha was troubled about many things because she wasn't focused on the one thing. If Martha could learn to give the one thing its proper place and priority, the many things would take care of themselves.

It's far too easy for us to live with the Many-Things Syndrome. Our lives are full. Eating and sleeping and working are just part of it. The rest of our hours are crammed with birthday parties and class presentations and yard chores and vacations and school events and car repairs.

My son graduated kindergarten awhile back, and the school organized a full-on graduation ceremony complete with caps and gowns. It lasted at least eight hours. On top of that we had our own after-party. I love my son, and he was adorable in his outfit—but at some point I found myself wondering, *Really? What are we celebrating here? You can't even flunk kindergarten. Do we really need another event?*

That's the world we live in, though. It's a nonstop succession of scheduling and organizing and double- or triple-booking ourselves. Our heroes are those who can juggle all the balls and balance all the plates and keep all the hoops spinning and tell jokes at the same time. They are the successful people. They are the ones to admire and emulate.

So we chatter on our hands-free phones as we maneuver through rush-hour traffic while we chain-drink chai lattes and listen to motivational CDs about how to multitask and speed-read. Then we complain that our brains hurt.

The ironic thing is that a lot of what we do is actually fun, or it would be if we could relax enough to enjoy it. Hopefully you enjoy your career and believe in what you're doing. Hopefully you love your offspring and even like them most of the time. Hopefully you have enough money to enjoy good food and go on vacations.

Life is awesome. It just moves so fast sometimes that we forget to enjoy it.

I don't mean to imply that all our busyness is our own choice. Often it's a result of circumstances beyond our control. Maybe that is your case right now: you find yourself trapped in a labyrinth of hard labor and hard choices. Peace is elusive not because your schedule is full of kids' parties and manicures and golf games, but because you are desperate to simply survive. Life for you has been a succession of storms that have left you worn and weary.

Whatever the "many things" might be that vie for your attention, Jesus is the one thing that is really needed. I don't know what your many things are, but I can promise you that Jesus does. And he wants to give each of us peace with ourselves and with him that will change us forever.

Martyr Martha

I want to take a closer look at the story we just read. When most of us first hear Martha's complaint, we totally get it. Our initial reaction is to high-five Martha. Martha is a hard worker. She shoulders her share of the load. She gets things done.

But Mary? Mary is a slacker. Mary is a freeloader. She sits around while there is work to be done.

Notice that what Martha is doing is not wrong. In fact, she is doing exactly what is expected of her. Martha is the older sister. She's the matron of the house. In this culture, she is the one who is expected to create an environment of rest for her guests. She's simply being a good host. She's doing what she is supposed to do.

I think that what Jesus is saying is that what we are expected to be doing is not necessarily what God wants us to be doing. Jesus seems to be implying to Martha, "I know you're doing what you're supposed to be doing, but sometimes you need to stop doing anything and just be with me."

Martha is doing the best she can. She is doing what she knows to do. Sometimes you'll hear people say, "Just do your best. That's all you can do. You know, do your best and let God do the rest."

But sometimes it's not about *doing* at all. It's about being with God, enjoying God, and having peace with God.

It's funny: Martha is upset because Mary is distracted from her responsibilities by Jesus. But Martha is distracted from Jesus by her responsibilities. Jesus is making a profound point—what we are distracted by says a lot about our value system.

There are many things clamoring for our attention. What distracts us? What holds our focus? What grabs our attention?

Is it our to-do lists? Is it our unanswered text messages and voice mails?

Or is it Jesus?

Busyness makes us feel important. It makes us feel needed. Martyrdom seems very noble. After all, someone has to be the responsible one, the organizer, the designated driver. The buck has to stop somewhere. It feels so good to be the one who holds the universe together.

Don't get me wrong. Responsibility and hard work are important. Planning ahead and taking ownership are important. But if we don't have the one thing in place, the many things will consume us. Like Martha, we'll find ourselves worried and troubled.

We can't cure the Many-Things Syndrome just by quieting ourselves or disciplining ourselves. I know, because I've tried. Maybe you have too.

Maybe it's in the morning, or late at night, and you get some time alone. You decide to pray and just enjoy God. But the moment you finally get still and quiet, along come all the thoughts you had forgotten about, the things you need to do, the people you need to answer, the decisions you need to make.

"I need to—oh, my gosh—I forgot that I have to—oh, and I also need to—" And there you are, five minutes into enjoying God, and you've got a list of things to do.

What do we do? How do we overcome this propensity? What's the answer? It's not by ignoring our pending projects and responsibilities. It's not by selling everything and buying a cabin in Montana. I'm not advocating a lifestyle of ignorance or irresponsibility.

The real problem isn't that we have a lot going on. Rather, it's the attitudes that these things produce in us: busyness, urgency, anxiety, worry, and stress. And the antidote is the peace that God gives.

When we have God's peace, the remaining priorities fall into place. We see more clearly. We discern what is important, what is urgent, what is unnecessary, and what is distracting.

The key to handling the distractions of life is to focus on Jesus, the source of peace. It is to sit at his feet like Mary did. It is to hear his heart, to know his love, to understand his priorities. It is to receive the peace he brings.

Shalom

Shortly before Jesus died, he gave his disciples a parting gift, the gift of peace. We read in the fourteenth chapter of the Gospel of John: "Peace I leave with you, My peace I give to you; not as the world gives do I give to you. Let not your heart be troubled, neither let it be afraid" (v. 27).

Notice the redundancy: "Peace I leave with you. My peace I give to you." Jesus wanted to emphasize this. He was telling his disciples, "Guys, listen up. This is a big deal. You need my peace, and it's available right now."

During this same conversation, Jesus told the disciples he was going back to heaven soon. If I were one of these young guys and had just heard that my hero and my mentor was going to disappear, I'm not sure I'd be excited about this parting gift. I'd be like, "Peace? I don't think that's enough. That doesn't make me feel any better here. Could we get something a bit more . . . substantial?"

When we are used to solving and fixing and building, peace can seem a little wimpy. It can feel irresponsible. It might even sound boring.

To us, peace usually means tranquility—maybe a still pond, a canoe, and a good book. Or maybe not a canoe. Canoes tip over. You get the picture though. Peace for us is happy thoughts, happy feelings, lack of conflict, lack of activity, calmness.

But the peace Jesus gives is "not as the world gives." In other words, this is not the typical peace that people imagine, with or without canoes.

The peace Jesus gives is far more substantial and effective and active than this world's peace. It is deep, profound, and lasting. It stays with us regardless of our external circumstances. It is more real and more powerful than the ups and downs of life.

In his teaching, Jesus was referring to a specific and incredibly poignant Hebrew word for which we have no English equivalent: *shalom.* "Peace" is the best translation we can come up with, but it doesn't begin to do justice to *shalom.*

Maybe you've heard the word *shalom.* Maybe you've heard Christians or someone in the Jewish community say it. Oftentimes it's used as a greeting or as a farewell. *Shalom* is an extraordinary concept in the Hebrew language.

Shalom means tranquility and peace, but it also means wholeness, soundness, completeness, prosperity, health. It goes far beyond just a warm sensation in your heart. It refers to complete, comprehensive well-being.

God's peace is first and foremost peace with him. It is an

internal, spiritual wellness that is the foundation for peace in every other area. When we have peace with God, we are able to find peace with ourselves, peace with others, and peace even in the turbulence of life.

It's important to realize when Jesus told his disciples that he was going to leave them shalom, he was making a massive theological statement. This wasn't a flippant, "Peace, dudes. See you later." Jesus was inaugurating a new way of relating to God.

If we had been raised under the terms of the Old Testament Law, we would understand that shalom is never present unless there is righteousness. Peace was a benefit of keeping the law.

God had given Israel a list of laws and rules that they had to follow perfectly in order to live at peace with him. The most famous of these are the Ten Commandments. If mankind failed to follow these rules, relationship with God was broken and peace was lost.

There was a big problem with this, though, because humanity was incapable of keeping all the commandments perfectly. That meant relationship with God was nearly non-existent. Israel related to God based on a complicated system of sacrifices, rituals, and laws. It was a temporary and insufficient solution that couldn't fully restore peace between God and humanity.

But God had promised that one day he would make a covenant of peace with his people. One day, peace would be restored. In the book of Isaiah, chapter 54, God declared to Israel, "For the mountains shall depart and the hills be removed, but My kindness shall not depart from you, nor shall My covenant of peace be removed" (v. 10).

Now, Jesus was telling his disciples that this covenant of peace had arrived. They could have shalom with God and shalom in life not through keeping the law, but through Jesus.

It's impossible to exaggerate the significance of this truth. Peace—that essential, elusive, universal need of mankind—is restored to us in the person of Jesus. The Ten Commandments couldn't save us and didn't save us and won't save us. We trust in Jesus, who did for us what we could not do for ourselves. Our trust is completely in him—not in our conduct, not in our qualifications, not in our background, not in our performance. We find our peace in his performance and perfection. The laws have been fulfilled. The case has been closed. Our righteousness is established and peace is restored.

Jesus is the way to peace with God. And this is not just a temporary, circumstantial peace. It's not a truce that lasts only as long as our good behavior. This is eternal, profound, life-altering peace. This is shalom with God, and it is Jesus' gift to us.

Peace Kisses

The Bible makes an amazing statement about righteousness and shalom in Psalm 85, verse 10: "Mercy and truth have met together; righteousness and peace have kissed."

The psalms were originally songs, so for centuries people

sang this song about mercy and truth meeting together and righteousness and peace kissing, but they could never figure out exactly how that would happen. Like a good indie song, the lyrics were catchy but ambiguous.

What did mercy have to do with truth? Mercy was messy and fuzzy and emotional; truth was cold and hard and factual. Truth analyzed our failures and demanded justice. Truth had no room for mercy. They were opposites, enemies, opponents in the ring.

Righteousness and peace had the same broken relationship. They hadn't been seen together since the garden of Eden. They hadn't even exchanged e-mails. "We Are Never Ever Getting Back Together" was their ringtone. But now righteousness and peace are making out? And mercy and truth are BFFs? What? When? How?

Jesus is the answer to the enigma. He brings them together in himself. Jesus is the embodiment of mercy and truth. Jesus is the living personification of righteousness and peace.

Without Jesus, we have no righteousness and therefore no shalom. But through him, we can enjoy true peace. It is his gift to us. We have spiritual peace with God, and we have peace in life. We can experience the abundance and wholeness and completeness that God created us to enjoy. The answer to condemnation, guilt, distraction, worry, and anxiety is the peace that comes through Jesus.

Remember what Jesus said to Martha? "You are worried about many things." Well, of course she was. She was a good Israelite. That was the hallmark of their existence. People who wanted to please God were constantly concerned with fulfilling laws and rules and expectations.

Then Jesus showed up and said, "I'm going to change everything. I don't want you to live busy, worried, anxious, and fearful. I'm ushering in a new era where just one thing is needed. Just enjoy me. Because in me, righteousness and peace have kissed. Mercy and truth have met together. I can do for you what fifteen hundred years of attempting to adhere to the Law cannot. Just sit down, Martha, and listen to me."

Busyness and distraction are a fact of our existence today. But when I read that shalom is available to me, I realize that my life can be different.

Paul writes in 2 Corinthians, chapter 5, that God "made Him who knew no sin to be sin for us, that we might become the righteousness of God in Him" (v. 21). We are righteous through faith in Jesus, and we have peace through faith in Jesus. Righteousness and peace go together. If we are righteous, we will have shalom. If we have shalom, it's because we are righteous.

Righteousness kisses peace in our lives, and peace kisses righteousness. We've been kissed. Our lives are now characterized by both righteousness and peace, and by both mercy and truth. It's not one or the other.

I don't know about you, but I don't feel very kissable. I don't deserve to be kissed by God. I've messed up so many times. But I'm righteous. I have shalom. How? Through grace. Through Jesus.

In Luke, chapter 15, how did the father greet his prodigal

son? He kissed him. Not because of what he had done—he kissed him despite what he had done. It's a picture of a new era, a new way of relating to God, one in which his acceptance, favor, shalom, blessing, love, and forgiveness will be perpetually upon us in spite of our performance and our waywardness.

We are continually kissed. Why? Because Jesus is our peace.

10

God in a Manger

They'll Never Do That Again

Parents are noble people, courageous people who deserve a lot of honor. And maybe medical attention.

Parents of multiple children deserve to be especially applauded. To use a sports analogy, parents of one child are playing a two-on-one game. It's double coverage. How great is that? The kid doesn't stand a chance. But some of us had a second child and had to switch to man-on-man coverage. That's more intense. The odds are about even. And then a brave few souls moved on to three or more kids, and now our only option is zone defense. Basically all hope is now lost. We are outnumbered and outwitted and outplayed.

Chelsea and I are parents of three offspring. I've noticed a consistent characteristic in parents who have produced three or more human beings: we tend to become desensitized. This is a fact. We become numb.

I can prove this to you. Just consider parents who have only one child. Notice their care, their concern, their protection. They are like two bodyguards flanking a celebrity. Every burp is cause for celebration. Other sounds too.

Our oldest son, Zion, was born prematurely and spent two weeks in the hospital. Those weeks were moving and precious and delicate and prayerful all at the same time.

I remember looking at him in the incubator. We held his little hand, and we prayed for him, and we tried to feed him enough bottles to get his weight up so they would let him out on parole. Once in a while we were able to hold him for a couple of minutes, and our hearts would melt.

Then finally, they gave us our child to take home. We took him out into the open ozone of earth. Then we strapped him into this metal machine that moved at high speeds. And we were thinking, *This is not right. This is dangerous.*

Then we got onto the freeway. I never had a problem keeping up with the flow of traffic until my firstborn son was in a seat in the back. Suddenly I found myself white-knuckling it in the slow lane, using explicit words at cars that were whizzing past.

Then Zion got a bit older and started to crawl and climb. He got up on things like railings and stairs and chairs. And if he got six inches off planet Earth, I was in a panic.

"Oh, my gosh, Zion, get down!"

And I would run to his aid, and I would rescue him in my strong arms, and I would hold him tenderly and kiss him all over.

Then we had another child. Attention lessened slightly. Parental consideration dwindled a bit.

And then we had a third. When she climbs things now, it's totally different. I've become so numb to the fragility of life. She climbs railings and chairs and stairs and I'm unconcerned and undisturbed. I can be sitting by a hotel pool and somebody asks, "Is that your daughter on the balcony on the fifth floor?"

I say, "Can you see her? Is she okay?"

"Well, she's walking on the railing."

"She's such a great gymnast." And then I yell up without even looking, "It's going to hurt if you fall!"

The other day our darling little girl touched the fireplace and burned her little finger. And these were the compassionate, endearing words of my wife: "Well, she'll never do that again."

With our firstborn, we would have rushed to the ER. We would have insisted they put our kid under general anesthesia and do surgery. "He's got a blister! You've got to save him!"

Now it's just, "Well, she'll never do that again." That is the recurring theme of parents with more than one child. "She's in the middle of the ocean with sharks? That's gonna hurt. Won't do that again."

We're numb. Completely desensitized. But the truth is, parents with one child are actually right. The way they care for their lone little nugget is appropriate and proper, because human beings are frail, finite, fragile creatures.

Sometimes, after a prolonged period of good health and financial success, we get fooled into thinking we are impervious to harm. We are unstoppable and gifted and on top of the world. It's the illusion of control.

But human beings are frail. How long can we last without

shelter? Or without food? Or without water? Or without air? Life would be over in a matter of minutes without these basic necessities.

The truth is, life is fragile. One glance at current news tells you this. Tragedy and harm and death are far too prevalent. We do as much as we can to protect our children, our finances, our future, and our possessions, but life is a vapor. Our security and our identity can be completely altered in a moment.

When we come face-to-face with this reality, we might be tempted to withdraw, to defend, to hedge our bets. Sometimes we just don't want to risk anymore. We don't want to attempt bold things anymore. We don't want to believe anymore. Sometimes we think our best option is to hunker down, hold on, and hope to preserve what we have.

But in the midst of our frailty and fragility, God wants to be our source of strength. We can have peace and confidence in life because God, the Creator of life, knows what we are going through.

God sees our weaknesses. He understands our uncertainties. He knows our needs. God is the perfect Father, and his care and concern for us never cease. In an insecure world, we are secure in his love. We can trust him.

God in a Manger

God proved his understanding of the frailty of mankind in the birth of Jesus. I think that's amazing. The way God entered the world reveals his heart for the world.

The Gospel of Luke, chapter 2, records the story of Jesus' birth:

> Joseph also went up from Galilee, out of the city of Nazareth, into Judea, to the city of David, which is called Bethlehem, because he was of the house and lineage of David, to be registered with Mary, his betrothed wife, who was with child. So it was, that while they were there, the days were completed for her to be delivered. And she brought forth her firstborn Son, and wrapped Him in swaddling cloths, and laid Him in a manger, because there was no room for them in the inn. (verses 4–7)

This passage tells us that God came to earth as a baby, and his crib was a manger. That was unexpected, to put it mildly. What was the all-powerful, all-knowing Creator of the universe doing in a feeding bowl for animals?

He is God. He had the right to choose how he was going to enter the world. He could ride in on a white horse or an F-16 fighter jet or a rainbow-colored space unicorn. But God chose the most peculiar surroundings, circumstances, and situations possible. It's exceptional. It's ridiculous, actually.

God picked a night in which every hotel, motel, and Holiday Inn was already booked. That wasn't an oversight. He didn't forget to reserve a room for Jesus. It was his plan. He wanted all normal accommodations to be full.

So Jesus was born in a stable. We usually imagine it as a barn, but it was most likely a cave. Jesus entered this world in a cave surrounded by an audience of smelly animals. His bed was a feeding trough used by all the animals, probably carved out of rock, which most likely had food remnants, saliva, and mud in it.

High on my long list of phobias and OCD triggers are animal hair and saliva. That's why I like dogs only from a distance. Once they start jumping up on me and slobbering and shedding, I'm out. That's where I draw the line. I know I said I'm desensitized and numb, but the thought of placing a newborn baby in the midst of so many germs gives me the chills.

Also, have you ever wondered what the animals did for food once Jesus was born? He was sleeping in their food dish. Joseph probably didn't sleep well for days, worrying that the animals might get confused at night.

If you look further in Luke's story, Jesus' first guests were shepherds.

Again, we are so far removed from this culture and this setting that we romanticize this. In my mind, the shepherds have color-coordinated outfits and neat little hipster beards, and they smell like Old Spice because somehow their sheep don't have normal bodily functions.

In reality, shepherds were the lowest of the low among society. They talked rough, looked rough, and smelled rough. Because shepherds lived out in the fields, they couldn't fulfill all the Jewish religious traditions and laws. They were considered ceremonially unclean and were typically not allowed to participate in temple worship. When normal, upstanding members of this ancient Jewish culture encountered shepherds, they held their breath and crossed the street.

But God was like, "When my Son is born, I want animals to be there. And I want shepherds to be there. And I want him to be born in a nowhere town. Oh, and just for fun—I want his mom to be a teenage girl."

Have you been around teenage girls lately? No offense if you happen to be a teenage girl, but I was a youth pastor for ten years, and the idea that a teenage girl would be the caretaker and nurturer for baby God is . . . surprising.

Because Mary got pregnant before Mary and Joseph were married, rumors that Jesus was illegitimate would follow him the rest of his life. And trying to blame the pregnancy on God would have just made Joseph look incredibly naive. I can only imagine the questions and sideways glances at family reunions for the next few decades.

What are you doing, God? What message are you trying to send us? A puzzled stepdad, a mystified teenage mom, smelly animals, a cave, antisocial shepherds, family dysfunction— what was going on in this nowhere town called Bethlehem? You could have arrived on the planet with royalty and renown, with parades and pomp and splendor. What are you trying to say, God?

We would have expected Jesus' birth to highlight the royalty of God. Instead, his birth highlighted the frailty of man.

It seems to me that God was intent on not skipping any risks when coming to this planet. He came to Earth in all its rawness and crudeness and pain, bent on facing the fragilities this life has to offer. Jesus identified fully with our weaknesses so that he could be our strength.

Maybe you wonder, *Does God care that I haven't had a pay-check for four months? Does God care that my spouse and I are on the verge of divorce? Does God see my worries and weak-nesses? Or is he so far above me and so far removed from me that these things don't matter?*

If you're wondering if God is interested in the idiosyncra-sies and the nuances of your everyday life, the answer is yes. God is keenly aware of our pain, our challenges, our difficul-ties, and our problems.

Just look at his first night on Earth. Just look at baby Jesus asleep in that carved-out feeding bowl. There's a message there.

And it's not just that life is fragile. It's that God is aware of our fragility, but he is bigger, and he is stronger, and he is with us. God is saying to us, "I know life is uncertain. But I'm not. I am with you always."

God isn't surprised or disappointed or bored when we feel overwhelmed. He knows us and cares about us more than anyone. He counts the number of hairs on our heads—how much more important are our struggles, our doubts, our desperation?

The good news is Jesus didn't just experience the frailty of life. He conquered it. He lived without sin so he could set us free from sin. He defeated the grave so we would never have to fear sickness or loss or death again.

The reason Jesus' birth is so important is his death. He was not born to live; he was born to die. And his death laid a sure foundation once and for all, a solid rock that outlasts all the fluctuations of our existence. Regardless of our circumstances, Jesus is life, Jesus is hope, and Jesus is peace.

Unexpected Hero

I wish there were a way to guarantee that nothing bad would ever happen. I wish I could guarantee that we would never experience grief or pain or loss. I wish I could protect myself and my family and those around me. We all do. But life gives us no such guarantees.

You've probably faced firsthand the frailty of life. Maybe you're going through terrible loss even now, or maybe you've been through it in the past. Maybe holidays are a painful reminder of a loved one you lost. Maybe you feel the bitterness of bankruptcy or the tearing pain of divorce. Maybe illness seems to be draining your life one day at a time.

I am not trying to be dramatic. These things are real. What are we going to do with the fragility of this life? How are we going to make it through the challenges and the mountains? How are we going to keep our heads? Optimism? The power of the human spirit?

No. Positive thinking and hard work and the human spirit are good, but they do not change the unpredictability of our existence.

How about faith? For those of us who consider ourselves Christians or Jesus-followers, can faith and trust and prayer and religion and good works save us from life's frailty?

Again, the answer is no. In themselves, these things have no power. Faith must be placed in something greater than itself. Don't put your faith in your faith or your trust in your trust. It sounds spiritual and religious, but it's nothing more than empty humanism.

People who put their trust in their anchor of faith are like a sailor in the middle of a storm who's admiring his anchor while his ship is bearing down on a rocky shoal.

"Come on, crew. Gather around! What do you think of my anchor? I just painted her."

"Captain, sir—permission to speak freely."

"Yes, sailor."

"We're going to die."

"I don't understand."

"There's a storm, sir. There are rocks ahead. Could we plunge the anchor into the abyss until it hits solid ground so that we can live?"

Faith is not to be admired. Faith is not a merit badge to show off. Faith is meant to be plunged into the abyss and the darkness of life's uncertainty until it anchors in a sure foundation and a solid Savior.

Our faith is in Jesus. It's not in community or in each other. It's not in programs or websites or songs. It's not in our social status, our health, our wealth, or our cleverness. None of these things are a guarantee of security or peace.

Our faith is in a person. He is the only sure thing in humanity. He is the only secure thing. David—the most famous of Israel's kings and heroes—wrote in Psalm 39, verses 4–7:

LORD, remind me how brief my time on earth will be.
Remind me that my days are numbered—
how fleeting my life is.
You have made my life no longer than the width of my
hand.
My entire lifetime is just a moment to you;
at best, each of us is but a breath . . .
And so, Lord, where do I put my hope?
My only hope is in you. (NLT)

David wanted to continually remember two things: first, how short and uncertain life is; and second, how strong and sure God is.

I love that final phrase: "My only hope is in you." Who is our only hope? Where do we put our anchor? What is our ultimate source of sanity, security, and peace? Jesus is our only hope. He's all we have and he's all we need.

When Jesus was born in the stable, the angels declared to the shepherds: "There is born to you this day in the city of David, a Savior" (Luke 2:11).

A Savior. Isn't that what we're looking for? We need a hero. We need a rescuer. Look at Hollywood's infatuation with superheroes. It's human nature to long for someone with supernatural ability to deliver us from the unpredictability and fragility of our existence.

The angels said, "He has arrived. He has been born. He is your Savior."

I doubt the shepherds expected their Savior to be so

vulnerable and frail. They probably imagined someone more like Thor: a ripped, thirtysomething, ready-made deliverer who would descend in splendor and sheer force to unleash peace upon the earth.

But Jesus' arrival was about as underwhelming as possible. He was born unplanned, unannounced, a misfit. He lived for years under the care of his very human mom and dad. He probably grew up making chairs and benches and tables in his dad's carpentry shop. He went through puberty like any other teenager. He lived life like you and me.

Why? Because there is a God who cares about the details of our lives, and he has faced the frailty of this planet and her people.

Jesus didn't just swoop in, save us, and soar back into the sky. He became us. He identified with us. He lived with us and loved us, and ultimately he died for us. He is our friend and our brother. He is our role model, our superhero, our Savior, our deliverer. But he became all these things by becoming weak like us.

Jesus faced life's fragility and frailty head-on. Now his victory and his constancy are our source of peace in every circumstance. We can depend on him. We can rest and rely on him. We can trust him.

First Place

Keeping Score

I am a slightly competitive person. I'm willing to admit it. This is especially the case when it comes to sporting events. Even with sports I usually couldn't care less about, once I engage in them, something kicks into gear and I get ridiculously, sometimes embarrassingly, competitive.

My competitiveness stems from the fact that I don't like losing. Losing is not an option. Some people tell me that when you lose, you learn valuable life lessons. I'd rather not learn those lessons. I'd rather be an ignorant winner than an enlightened loser.

This is why the modern concept of children's sports is absolutely mind-boggling to me. When I was growing up, no matter what game you were playing or how old you were, you kept score. The score was important because it told you who was the winner and who was the loser.

Today, though, children's egos have apparently become more fragile. We must protect their delicate self-esteem by telling them that they are all winners just because they showed up and tried hard. Keeping score at young ages is politically incorrect.

I fundamentally disagree with that entire notion and philosophy. That's why I'm training my children to beat yours.

When my boys were six and four, they signed on the dotted line to play T-ball for the Seattle River Dogs. You haven't heard of River Dogs? Strange.

My boys got their uniforms and hats and cleats, and they were excited to be River Dogs. Sometime during this process, someone informed me that there would be no one keeping score.

I was like, "What's the point of playing then?"

That didn't go over well.

But I could see what was going to happen. My boys would get dressed, they would lace up their cleats, they would swing their little hearts out at a ball perched on a rubber tee, and at the end of an hour and a half of this madness, no one would know what happened, because no one would be keeping score. Then they would all get a Capri Sun and a Nature Valley granola bar, and they would be told that they are all winners.

But they are not all winners. This is ridiculous to me. Go ahead, kids. Suck on your Capri Sun and enjoy your granola bar; but somebody needs to tell somebody who won and who lost.

So before their first game, I sat my boys down. I said, "Boys, you need to understand something. At the end of your T-ball games, no Smith child is going to be hopping up into my SUV, talking like, 'Dad, we won,' when you didn't win. So maybe nobody else will be keeping score, but I will. I'm not going to make a spectacle of it, and I'm going to be cool, calm, and collected; but I'm going to be counting the runs. And when you get in the car, I will tell you if you won or if you lost.

"So if you come and you're all happy, sucking on your Capri Sun, talking about how you won, I'm going to say, 'No, you didn't win. In fact, you got crushed.' And if the other team talks about how they won when really they lost, I'm going to say to you, 'Those kids did not win. You are faster. You are bigger. You are stronger. And you crushed them.' "

It's not just in scorekeeping that parents and coaches and leagues have gotten a bit soft. The entire experience is remarkably noncompetitive.

A player steps up to the plate, faces the ball, and swings. The ball is stationary, remember, but somehow he hits the rubber tee eight inches below the ball. It trickles off and rolls a couple of feet, and the coach starts yelling, "Run! Run! You hit it!"

No he didn't. He missed it. He knocked out the ball's support, and gravity did the rest.

So the kid runs, and the other team throws the ball in the general direction of first base. The first baseman can't catch, of course. So the batter, after looking confused for a minute because the parental shouting is out of control, takes off for second. The other team is still looking for the ball behind first base, so the batter runs to third. Then he runs home and the coach is like, "A home run!"

A home what? That was not a home run. That was a strike.

As I said, I am slightly competitive. I want first place. I want to win. And I suppose that has both helped me and hurt me in life.

I think there should be a passion in our hearts to be excellent. In fact, I think that's part of being human. I think there's something innate in our DNA that wants to win, and I think that desire comes from God, the ultimate champion of the ages. God is a winner, and we were made in his image and likeness.

But I think our desire to be first can hurt us in some areas, because in the kingdom of God, there is a bit of a paradox centered on this concept of being first. Here's the paradox: the key to getting ahead in life is being behind or being second place in God's kingdom. As long as we are behind, we will be ahead.

Jesus needs to take the wheel, as Carrie Underwood pointed out a few years back. We need to be comfortable riding shotgun for the rest of our lives.

God is forever first and foremost. The sooner we realize that and the sooner we implement it in our daily lives, the sooner we will find ourselves getting ahead in life. Our destiny is to be ahead in life by being behind Jesus. Jesus is first.

In the Beginning

The last book of the Bible has a lot to say about the firstness of Jesus. *Firstness* is a word, in case you were wondering. Some of you overachievers were about ready to look it up. I know your kind. I'm married to one, actually. I checked on the infallible and inerrant Internet, and *firstness* means things like "the quality of being first, in-itselfness, originality, primacy, and precedence."*

In Revelation, chapter 1, verse 8, we read: "'I am the Alpha and the Omega—the beginning and the end,' says the Lord God. 'I am the one who is, who always was, and who is still to come—the Almighty One'" (NLT).

Firstness—and lastness—are defining characteristics of Jesus. He is first because he is God, and he is God because he is first. By the way, *alpha* and *omega* are the first and last letters of the Greek alphabet. Jesus is saying, "I am your A to Z. I am the start and the finish." And by implication, he is everything in between. In other words, Jesus was here before us, he's here with us, and he'll be here long after we're gone.

A few verses later, Jesus says it again. "Don't be afraid! I am the First and the Last. I am the living one. I died, but look—I am alive forever and ever! And I hold the keys of death and the grave."

Jesus is first and Jesus is last. His lastness is also an amazing concept, but I want to focus here on the implications and ramifications of his firstness.

God is first theologically. He is first socially. He is first

---

* "the condition of being first": www.collinsdictionary.com/dictionary /english/firstness. "The quality of being first; originality; priority" (also mentions in-itselfness): en.wiktionary.org/wiki/firstness. "Being before all others with respect to time, order, rank, importance, etc.": dictionary .reference.com/browse/firstness. The definition of *firstness* according to Merriam-Webster Online is "a fundamental category in Peircean philosophy comprising qualities like redness, hardness, bitterness, and nobility and expressive of possibility, spontaneity, and chance—compare." Go figure.

physically and psychologically and anthropologically. He is first in everything, everywhere, all the time.

I believe that many of the complexities in our lives correlate directly to our inability to grasp God's firstness. The answer for our fears and worries and anxieties is to understand God is first. The answer for our marriages, the answer for our parenting, the answer for our friendships is to keep Jesus in first place.

Being second is the key to our lives. Often, the intricacies and difficulties we face come because we have taken first place. We are holding the steering wheel. And because we are in first place, complexity, anxiety, fear, strife, and stress ensue.

There is simplicity in grace and the gospel. There is simplicity in Jesus. He is first. He is in control. He loves us, and he has a plan and a future for us.

It's challenging for any of us to yield control to Jesus, but I think it's especially hard for people who are gifted and talented and have it all together. If we have never been the smartest, brightest, best, or fastest at anything, then it's a bit easier to look to God for help, because we already know we aren't in control. But if we're used to success, if we have degrees and titles and influence and power, sometimes it's hard to remember that God is before us.

It's not that we have to make him first. He already was first and always will be first. This is about recognizing that he is first on a practical, tangible level. It is about living mentally and emotionally and socially with God in first place.

Nothing about God will ever be second. He plays second

fiddle to no one. He is God all by himself. He was not voted in and he can't be voted out. He does not need the recognition of men to remain God. He will continue to function and rule as God whether mankind realizes and responds or not. He is God of the ages. He is God of every generation. He is God of every country, of every planet, and of every star suspended in the sky.

So when we presume to tell God what to do and how to run our lives, it's just a tiny bit ridiculous.

The amazing thing is that God does give us a lot of control. He gives us a free will; he gives us resources to manage; he gives us a life span to administrate and enjoy. But he is still sovereign. He is still first. What does that mean for us?

Here we are, stressed out about the bills that are due. Yet we have on our side the God who is the first and the last, the Alpha and the Omega, the beginning and the end. That changes everything.

Because there is nothing second about God, there is nothing second about Jesus. Jesus is the express image of God, and Jesus is God.

Jesus existed first. Jesus lived a sinless life first. Jesus conquered death first. Jesus is first in all things for all time.

This realization should relieve the pressure that some of us live under constantly. If you're a follower of Jesus, the pressure isn't on you. It's on Jesus. Put your cares, your concerns, your worries, and your fears on the one who is first.

"Jesus, I trust you. Jesus, I look to you and wait for you."

When you wake up in the dark hours of the morning, don't consider first the difficulties of the day ahead. When you feel a twinge in your back, don't consider first your age or your medical history. When a bill is due, don't consider first your limitations and lack.

Before you do anything else, consider Jesus. Look at Jesus. Think about Jesus.

The answer to many of our problems is simple: it's thinking about Jesus more than ourselves. Jesus has to be first on a practical, emotional level—not just a mental agreement level—or complexity and fear and anxiety will begin to control our minds and hearts.

I am frequently guilty of making myself first. Actually, I've been a prodigy, from a very young age, at considering myself first. No one had to teach me or train me to do it. I was born with an immense capacity to think about myself first in every situation and circumstance.

Imagine what our lives would look like if Jesus were first in everything. If he were the first thing we considered in everything. If he were the first person we vented to in every situation and circumstance. If he were our knee-jerk reaction.

Imagine if every time tragedy threatened, our automatic, immediate response was to think, *First, I've got to go to Jesus. First, I've got to talk to Jesus. First, I've got to trust Jesus. First, I've got to cast my cares on Jesus. Jesus is my source. Jesus is my answer.*

That is far better than, *I've got to make some phone calls. I've got to send some e-mails. I've got to fix the problem and figure this out. I've got to have the answers right now, for everything and everyone, or everything will fall apart.*

When we keep Jesus first, the rest of life falls into place. Our stress level drops. Our pulse slows back down. The fear that paralyzed us evaporates, and we are free to evaluate and prioritize and maneuver through the speed bumps of life.

More and Before

One of the implications of Jesus' firstness is that he is *more*. To be first implies that you have more or are more of something. You are more qualified or more able; therefore, you are first.

When my boys beat the other T-ball team, it was because they had more skill, more speed, or more talent. More makes you first, and if you are first, it's because you are more.

Jesus is always more. More than what? I'll let you fill in the blank. Think of the most astronomical thing you can, and Jesus is more. He's more than bankruptcy. More than sickness. More than sin. More than murder. More than divorce. More than tragedies, tsunamis, wars, or famines.

Jesus is more than the darkest season of your soul. Jesus is more than your weakness. He's more than your problems. He's more than your finiteness.

What are you facing? He's more.

What are you worried about? He's more.

Jesus never fails. There is nothing in this life or the life to come that could alter the moreness of Jesus. He transcends and supersedes. He overcomes and outlasts. Jesus is more.

A second implication of Jesus' firstness is that he is *before*.

This is especially important to remember when we are going through times of grief and difficulty.

When things are going well, we forge forward naturally. But when tragedies and problems come, we often want to stop advancing and just hide from life. We too easily find ourselves paralyzed by pain and fear.

"How can I keep moving in light of what happened? I want to stay bitter. I want to stay hurt. I want to stay in grief." It hurts too bad to get up and move forward. It's too hard to believe for better days.

The only way we can get up, collect our emotions, and trust God is to realize that if he's first, he's before us. He's already preparing a way ahead of us.

In Mark, chapter 14, when Jesus told his disciples that they were going to fail him and deny him, he said something interesting: "After I have been raised, I will go before you to Galilee" (v. 28). In other words, Jesus was planning and preparing a way for them after the darkest season of their lives.

Peter replied, "Even if all are made to stumble, yet I will not be."

I love Peter. He's a classic human being. That's how we usually think when things are going well.

"I'm not going anywhere. I will not stumble. I'm going to be all right. Everything's going to work out for me."

The truth is, there may be some challenges in your future. I'm not trying to discourage you, but it's important to be prepared mentally and emotionally and spiritually for those moments when we find ourselves stumbling.

The Bible says in Romans 8:28 that "all things work together for good to those who love God, to those who are the called according to His purpose." That verse doesn't mean everything will be easy. It doesn't mean everything will feel good. There might be times when you wonder why things look so dark and why God isn't anywhere in sight. But at the end of your life, when all the pluses and minuses and ups and downs have played out, the end result will be this: God is good, and he actively works all things together for good.

Jesus replied to Peter: "This night, before the rooster crows twice, you will deny Me three times" (Mark 14:30).

When I read this, I think, *Jesus, why tell him? Why make his discouragement worse?* Jesus had his reasons.

Fast-forward to chapter 16. It was the morning of the resurrection. Several women went to see the grave of Jesus, and an angel appeared to them.

He told them, "Do not be alarmed. You seek Jesus of Nazareth, who was crucified. He is risen! He is not here. See the place where they laid Him. But go, tell His disciples—and Peter—that He is going before you into Galilee; there you will see Him, as He said to you" (verses 6–7).

The angel mentioned Peter by name. It was a message from Jesus to a disciple who was stumbling, a man who was hiding in his hurt and shame.

"Peter, I'm not mad at you. I haven't given up on you. I knew what you were going to do. Remember? That's why I told you beforehand. But I've gone before you, and I'm making a way for you to come back to me."

Why did Jesus tell Peter he would fail? Because he wanted Peter to know that far more significant than his failure was the fact that Jesus is first and Jesus is before.

No offense, but God knew the dumb things you and I were going to do in our lives long before we did them. He knew about the damaged relationships. He knew about the secret sins. He knew about the crazy financial issues. He knew, because he is before. But he's not mad, and he's not frustrated, and he hasn't given up.

Too often we focus on our failures, on our tragedies, and on our pain, and we forget that Jesus is before all of that. Jesus saw our present back when it was the future, and he went on ahead of us to get things ready. Not only is Jesus with us in our pain, but he was here long before we got here, and he is preparing a way to bring us back.

I don't know what tomorrow holds. Ultimately, as I said, I know God is good and he works things out for our good. But you may have some difficult times. You may have some valleys. I don't know—but God does.

Here we are today, but he's already in our tomorrow. He's ensuring that no matter what dumb things we might do or what horrible things might happen to us, everything will work together for good.

Blue-Eyed Grace

Several years into my dad's fight with cancer, God said something very specific to me. I don't mean to sound spooky or superspiritual, but the words, though not audible, were close to it.

It happened while I was in my living room one day.

"You're going to have a third child, and it will be a baby girl. You will name her Grace. And you will always know my grace is sufficient for you. No matter what happens with your dad, you'll always know my grace is sufficient."

I told Chelsea that night, "Babe, I think I heard from God. We're going to have a baby girl." And I told her the story.

She said, "Wow." She probably said something more profound than that, but that's what I remember.

Sure enough, we got pregnant. And by *we*, I mean *she*, but it's politically correct to refer to pregnancy as a team experience.

A few months into the pregnancy, we discovered that it was a baby girl. You can imagine the emotion and the joy. And of course her birth a few months later was one of the highlights of our lives. We named her Grace, but we call her Gracie.

I mentioned earlier how relaxed third-time-around parents are. We took Gracie to church at the ripe old age of one day. She was in the back of the room with her grammy, and I think my dad as well, and they were *ooh*-ing and *ahh*-ing over this baby girl and her blue eyes.

At some point, though, something came over me, and I just knew, *I've got to go hold my little girl.* I can't explain it to you. It was like I had this strong sense that I had to go see her.

I went back and got Gracie, and we went into a room behind the stage. I closed the door behind me. It was just my brand-new little girl and me.

And as I sat there and gazed at her tiny, tender face, I lost it. I started crying uncontrollably. I looked at this baby girl, and I realized she was the tangible, visible manifestation of God's beforeness, his moreness, and his firstness.

I believe God is a healer, and I know that he does things that are far beyond what humans can do. So I hope what I'm about to say doesn't disrupt your faith. It didn't shake my faith at all.

As I stood in that room, holding my little girl, somehow I knew that my dad's days were short. I just knew. And I wept and I grieved, not really understanding what was happening. But somehow, in my grieving there was solace and faith. As I said, I can't explain it. I don't even understand all of it. But at that moment I knew that my God was more and before.

That day, I didn't have any idea what tomorrow would hold for our family and for our church. I didn't know that my dad's health would soon deteriorate rapidly, and that we would find ourselves living in crisis mode day after day. I didn't know that within a few months he would leave this life and find his ultimate healing in heaven.

But God did.

The pain I went through with my dad's death was beyond difficult. It was a pain I'd never experienced in my whole life. I didn't know how to function, how to keep going, or how to process what I felt.

So God sent me a little girl to remind me every day, *My grace is sufficient for you.* Every day, when I held my little girl and looked in her big blue eyes, I realized I was going to make it. I was going to be all right.

"Son, I'm going to be your source. I'm going to be your strength. I know the pain you're about to go through, so I'm making preparations so you can keep going. I'm going before you."

And he did. As I look back at that season in our lives, I can see God's hand throughout the process, working things together for my good and for the good of our family and church. He never left us; he never abandoned us; he never gave up on us.

Someday, I'm going to tell Gracie this story and she's going to realize the miraculous gift her life is. Among many other things, she is a constant reminder that even though my dad is gone, my heavenly Father is with me wherever I go, and I'm going to make it.

Whatever pain, whatever problem, or whatever sin you're facing; whatever your past or present or future holds—Jesus is more and he is before. Jesus is the first and he's the last. He's the Alpha and he's the Omega. He's the beginning and he's the end.

You and I, we can keep going. We can keep believing. We can keep trusting. The best is yet to come.

12

I Am Willing

Hanitizer

I am obsessed with hand sanitizer. True story. I absolutely love the stuff. Whenever I see hand sanitizer, I cannot help but utilize it. If I notice that you have sanitizer, I won't ask—I will just take some.

My wife realized this recently and felt obligated to point it out. I'm going to choose to believe she was laughing with me.

You might recall the swine flu panic a few years ago. It was ultimately underwhelming, but on the positive side, it motivated people to mount hand sanitizer dispensers on walls everywhere. My favorite kind is the motion-activated dispenser. All you have to do is wave your hand under it to get a shot of foamy emotional stability. It's glorious.

My poor kids bear the brunt of my obsession. We'll walk by these public dispensers, and I'll grab their hands and force them under the spout. "Take some. Wipe it all over your body. You're dirty."

When Gracie was four, she had heard about hand sanitizer so much that it became part of her vocabulary. She shortened it to the much more awesome *hanitizer*, and henceforth and forever it shall be known as hanitizer in the Smith household.

I don't know why I'm like this. Maybe it was how I was raised. I like to be clean. I like to feel like I'm protected. I like to feel like I'm at peace. And for whatever reason, hand sanitizer does that for me. I'm man enough to own up to that. When I put it on, I feel like Batman putting on his suit. Hanitizer and I can conquer the world.

I tried to explain this to Chelsea, and she just said, "What is wrong with you?"

I said, "Where do you want me to start?"

Sometimes I wonder, though—how do we know this stuff works? How do we know it kills 99.9 percent of the germs? Is someone counting the tiny corpses? And the scariest part: What about the 0.1 percent that is strong enough to survive? Those little guys are invisible, unstoppable, and coming for us. That's enough to scare anyone.

Recently a nice lady told me, "You know, these germs are building up antibodies, and eventually this stuff won't work. And as a result, you'll be even more susceptible to sickness. So this is probably working against you."

Thank you. I did not need to hear that.

Frankly, hand sanitizer works fine for me on an emotional

level. What's more important than that? When it comes to germs and microbes and bacteria, hanitizer is my source of peace.

The Law and the Leper

Fear of germs, however, doesn't come close to conveying the reaction of the people of Jesus' day to the dreaded disease of leprosy. Leprosy had religious and social implications that made lepers complete outcasts.

Lepers were not at peace in any sense of the word. Culturally, theologically, and emotionally, they were the epitome of everything unclean and unholy.

Leprosy was a living symbol of sin. Israelites in those days felt that if you had leprosy, it was likely a curse from God for the sins you had committed. It was horrible. It was deplorable. It was loathsome. And it was highly contagious.

The term *leprosy* in the Bible was used for many skin diseases, but they all caused the flesh to be eaten away. It was a feared, disfiguring condition. It was painful and humiliating and usually incurable.

Leviticus 13 and 14 describe the procedures and laws God instituted to protect people from the spread of leprosy. If you want a good read, check out these two chapters. They are fantastic. I'm kidding. They are gross. They say, among other things, that priests had to inspect any weird spots or growths that appeared on people's bodies to see if they were leprosy.

Suffice to say, I wouldn't have been a pastor back in those days. They didn't have hand sanitizer.

The laws in relationship to leprosy specified, among other things, that those who contracted it had to be completely removed from society. Whether they were married or not, whether they had kids or not, they were isolated and banished to leper colonies outside of town. It was total rejection. They were alive, but they were dead. They had lost their lives as they knew them.

The eighth chapter, verses 1–4, of Matthew describes an encounter between Jesus and one of these outcasts.

> Large crowds followed Jesus as he came down the mountainside. Suddenly, a man with leprosy approached him and knelt before him. "Lord," the man said, "if you are willing, you can heal me and make me clean."
>
> Jesus reached out and touched him. "I am willing," he said. "Be healed!" And instantly the leprosy disappeared. Then Jesus said to him, "Don't tell anyone about this. Instead, go to the priest and let him examine you. Take along the offering required in the law of Moses for those who have been healed of leprosy. This will be a public testimony that you have been cleansed." (NLT)

It's important to realize this takes place right after the most famous sermon ever preached: the Sermon on the Mount, found in Matthew, chapters 5 through 7.

You may or may not be familiar with the Sermon on the Mount, but I'm sure you're reasonably familiar with some of the principles and statements found there. For instance, what we now call the golden rule—"do unto others as you would have them do unto you"—is straight from this sermon. Entire cultures and societies have adopted and adapted ethical principles from the Sermon on the Mount.

Scholars believe Jesus might have taught for two or three days straight. That has to be some sort of record.

Eventually Jesus concluded his sermon. Matthew points out that Jesus then headed down the mountain. Why mention that detail? I don't believe it was an accident. I think he was drawing a parallel that Jewish readers would have understood. Moses gave Israel the ancient laws regulating leprosy. They were part of the Law of Moses, which as I mentioned earlier was the legal basis for Israel to maintain relationship with God. The Law was given to Moses on a mountain.

While Moses was on the mountain, however, the nation of Israel got impatient. They thought Moses must have died on the mountain. They said, "Moses is taking too long. So we have a great idea. Let's pool all our jewelry together, melt it down, make a big golden cow to worship, take our clothes off, and run around the camp, singing and playing wild music."

Moses showed up just as Woodstock was at its craziest. He was so outraged by Israel's actions that he threw down the stone tablets containing the Ten Commandments and they broke. Then he literally ground the golden cow to powder, mixed it with water like a protein drink, and made the people swallow it.

Contrast that story with Jesus' encounter here in the eighth chapter of Matthew. Jesus has just been on a mountain, teaching a new way of life and of relating to God that is based not on laws written on stone but on a relationship birthed in the heart. Now Jesus descends the mountain and encounters the embodiment of sin: a leper. But the story doesn't end the way the people of Israel would have expected.

It would be right for Jesus to be enraged. That was how Moses reacted to the law being broken. This leper is flaunting the law by coming to Jesus and mingling with healthy, clean people. If Jesus were to rebuke, threaten, and humiliate this man, people would think nothing of it. They would jump in on Jesus' side.

But instead of judgment, instead of breaking things and making people drink the punishment for their sin, Jesus comes down from his mountain, and he puts the broken pieces of this man's life back together. Ultimately, Jesus even takes the punishment for the leper's sins upon himself.

Jesus is the new Moses. He came to bring true peace between God and mankind. Jesus introduced a new era, a new walk with God, and a new way to be human.

We'll look at this more, but first, I want to take at look at Jesus' message on the mountain. It frames for us the significance of this interaction between Jesus and the leper.

Field Trip

The Sermon on the Mount is, as we've already established, the greatest sermon ever preached. It's beautiful, it's awesome, it's spellbinding, and it's extraordinary. But it's also discouraging.

If you read it closely and take it to heart, you'll realize something depressing. The Sermon on the Mount is unequivocally, unquestionably, 100 percent impossible for us to achieve and fulfill.

For instance, Jesus is like, "The law says you shall not commit adultery. But I say that if you've looked at a woman and lusted for her in your heart, you have already done the deed."

In other words, being a virgin isn't enough. You have to be completely free from lust, or you are no better off than the biggest player around.

That pretty much eliminates everyone right off the bat. If you're hanging your hat on the big V, you read that and suddenly you're discouraged. That was your claim to fame, your trump card of spirituality. Now you realize it's not enough.

It gets worse. Jesus lets loose a string of these impossible statements, and then concludes with this demotivating zinger: "Guys, bottom line: be as perfect as God. See you next Sunday. Thanks for coming."

You can look up *perfect* in the original language if you want—it means perfect. It's impossible to overestimate how hopeless this standard is.

God, what are you saying? What's the point?

It's the same point the entire Bible communicates. We need Jesus.

The people could never, no matter how hard they tried, fulfill the law. There was no peace. They were at odds with God.

They were unclean, and they could never make themselves clean.

The point of Jesus' sermon was not, "Now, go down the mountain and be perfect by yourselves. You're on your own. Work it out. Try harder." Jesus' message was, "I am the source of your holiness, of your cleanness, of your righteousness before God."

In order to find peace with God, we don't need to try harder. We need Jesus.

Jesus finishes the greatest sermon in human history, and then he says, "Let's go on a field trip. Allow me to demonstrate to you exactly what I mean."

The audience descends the mountain with Jesus, and at the base of the mountain is the very living symbol of sin. This is not an accident. This is a field trip divinely orchestrated by God.

Remember, this man with leprosy is blatantly breaking the law. He needs to be with the other lepers. He can't be this close to clean people because he is unclean. So when the crowd rounds the corner on the trail and encounters this man, chaos ensues. "Back! Everybody back! It's a leper!" Parents grab their kids. A few people pick up rocks in case the leper is aggressive or maybe insane.

The man certainly expected that reaction, but I doubt he ever became immune to it. What human could? He was rejected, isolated, broken.

Jesus doesn't flinch, though. He doesn't fall back. He doesn't get angry. If anything, he looks emotionally moved.

The man falls to the ground in desperation. He addresses Jesus: "Lord, if you are willing, you can make me clean."

Jesus does the unthinkable. He reaches out his hand and touches the man. "I'm willing. Be healed. Be clean."

When was the last time anyone had touched him? Some say a person can go clinically insane if he or she goes for a prolonged period of time without human touch. It is a fundamental human need, and this man had lived for maybe years without it.

Jesus didn't need to touch him in order to heal him. The very next story in Matthew's gospel shows Jesus healing a paralytic without even seeing him personally. Jesus is making a point.

Imagine what the onlookers are thinking. *This doesn't— wait—but he's unclean. The law—what are we doing here?*

Remember, in the sermon recorded in Matthew 5, Jesus had told the crowd: "Do not think that I came to destroy the Law or the Prophets. I did not come to destroy but to fulfill" (v. 17). Now he's proving it. He's demonstrating what he meant.

According to Leviticus, when something ceremonially unclean was touched by something clean, the clean thing became unclean. It's a lot like germs. If I have clean hands and touch something dirty, it doesn't mean the dirty object becomes clean. It just means I have to go find more hand sanitizer.

Jesus touches the leper, and instantly and miraculously, his leprosy disappears. For the first time in human history, something clean has made something that was unclean become clean again. Peace has been restored. Wholeness has been recovered.

In Jesus, everything has changed. The crowd can't help

but see it. First Jesus taught it; now he models it. The message of leprosy is that sin contaminates and spreads and infects. The message of Jesus is that he is greater than sin.

Jesus is demonstrating the gospel. He is modeling a new way to live. Jesus has conquered sin and sickness and death. Grace has nothing to fear from sin because grace overpowers sin. It heals the sinner. It restores the broken pieces. It removes the punishment. Now that Jesus is on the scene, sin and evil and guilt are on the run.

Jesus is like a walking, talking, teaching, loving dispenser of hanitizer. Sin has no power over him. Sickness can't stop him. Evil doesn't faze him. In a contaminated world, Jesus is the peace and stability and cleanness that people everywhere are looking for.

I don't know about you, but I'm not interested in going through life as scared of sin as I am of germs. I'm not planning to hunker down and hide out and hope evil stays away.

I'm excited about grace. I'm excited about mercy and love and this new way of relating to God. Grace plays offense. Grace takes the initiative to bring healing to the broken. Grace reaches out and embraces those who feel lonely, rejected, and desperate.

Let's not spend another day of our lives afraid of wickedness, or evil, or sin, or darkness. Let's not spend our time dissecting and deliberating how bad society has become. Instead, let's focus on the one who is greater than all the evil and darkness: Jesus. Let's focus on his goodness and his grace and his finished work.

It doesn't matter who you are or how long you've been

following Jesus. If Jesus is inside you, if grace has transformed you, then you are a force to be reckoned with. Guilt no longer has a hold on you. Condemnation no longer paralyzes you. Fear no longer controls you.

In Jesus, you and I are at peace, and we are carriers of peace. We are free to take the power of good, the power of grace, the power of Jesus to people who are desperate for it.

I Am Willing

The crowd following Jesus is barely off the mountain when they are confronted with what I believe is the essence of the whole sermon: a leper who, in a very real sense, represents every person there.

The leper is never named, because every man, woman, boy, and girl jumping back in horror is that man. I am that man. And—dare I say it?—you are that man.

Jesus is trying to show us something. This man has a diabolical disease that is literally eating him alive. It is disfiguring him. It is grotesque. It is deplorable. It is loathsome.

I believe Jesus is saying, "You think this external disease is bad? You have far worse on the inside. Your diabolical disease is eating you alive. It's called sin, and you're dying, and you need to be given new life. But I've come down my mountain to put broken things back together. I've come down my mountain, not to afflict you with the punishment you deserve, but to drink your punishment so that I can give you new life. I want to heal you so that you can reengage with relationships, and society, and purpose, and meaning."

This man has run out of options. He can't fix himself or save himself or cleanse himself. The leper hadn't even heard the sermon. He hadn't even made it to church that Sunday, so to speak. He is ceremonially unclean. He is the embodiment of unholiness. According to religion and law, he has no right to approach Jesus, much less ask for healing.

But he isn't looking for more religion. He isn't risking everything to engage with the law. He is searching for Jesus. He turns to Jesus. "Lord, if you're willing, you can make me clean. You can put me back together. I know you can."

We already read Jesus' response, but let me repeat it. He speaks some of the most compassionate, beautiful, hopeful, glorious words ever spoken on this planet: "I am willing."

He is saying to humanity everywhere: "I know how bad it is. I know how deplorable it is. I know how disfigured and displaced and lonely you are. I know the depth of your darkness. I see the secret shame. And I am willing and able to heal. I am willing and able to cleanse and restore."

What is required? Nothing but surrender. Nothing but the realization that we are out of options. That great crowd must have stood there until realization sank in. "Wow! This must be the point of Jesus' sermon. It's not about how holy we are or how perfect we are. It's about Jesus."

Jesus is the greater Moses. He is the fulfillment of the law. He has come down from heaven to help broken humanity. He has come to put us back together by his grace and mercy.

He has come because his love for humanity knows no end. It is unstoppable. It is unconditional. It is unrelenting. It is illogical.

Jesus brings peace to humanity: peace with God, peace with self, peace with others. He removes the barriers of sin and shame and uncleanness. Jesus is our peace.

LIFE IS to enjoy God.

I've said it throughout this book: God created life to be enjoyed. He wants us to have fulfilled, satisfied, happy, healthy lives.

Here's the best part. Enjoying life and enjoying God go hand in hand. If fact, they are inextricably connected. We won't fully enjoy life unless we learn to enjoy God; and if we enjoy God, we will absolutely love life.

God is the constant in the equation of our existence. He is the reason life works. He is the Creator of life, he is the giver of life, and he is the sustainer of life.

When it comes to enjoying each moment, God is on our side. He is not a divine downer, a cosmic party pooper, or a galactic grinch. God is the essence of fun. He is the embodiment of joy. He is the reason we love roller coasters and chocolate and knock-knock jokes.

God enjoys life. He always has and he always will. And he wants to enjoy it with you.

13

Enjoying God

The Formal Living Room

I grew up in a rather rough neighborhood. We had bars on all the doors and windows because our house had been robbed multiple times. We didn't have a lot of square footage, so we made good use of every room. We even dug out a basement.

When I turned thirteen, we moved into a larger house. And it was then that I was introduced to what is known as a formal living room.

Now, let me explain what this is to a generation that is unfamiliar with the concept. A formal living room is a space in your home that is not actually used for living. Don't be fooled by the name. It's just for looking.

I remember as a thirteen-year-old feeling deep consternation that we were setting apart a section of our new home for no one. In the upcoming years, if my sister or I, or a friend, or neighbor children somehow accidentally meandered into the no-go zone, we were immediately apprehended and physically dealt with.

The formal living room was uniquely and exclusively something to look at. Perfect vacuum lines were to always be engraved in the carpet, unmarred by human footsteps. Pillows were to be delicately fluffed. Furnishings were always to be color coordinated. It was the formal living room. No one dared to actually live life in the formal living room—that was unthinkable.

To emphasize its secluded, aloof, holy-of-holies status, my mom eventually had French doors built at the entrance to the formal living room. And then she put in a security system with cameras and lasers. It was crazy. (Okay, I might have made up that last part.)

I have kids of my own now, and the concept of a formal living room is starting to make sense to me. Chelsea and I don't have one, but I understand the motivation. I think the reason my mom had a formal living room is because she had children. And children have a way of making you feel like you're out of control—like confusion and chaos have taken over your life.

I think sometimes mom would steal away when none of us were looking, and she'd just look at the formal living room and think to herself, *I'm in control. I'm in charge. I'm normal. Look at the vacuum lines in the carpet. I'm on top of the world.*

It was like therapy. We all need that from time to time.

Eating on the Couch

The formal living room is a great metaphor for the way many of us relate to God. We admire him from a distance, but we don't live life with him or enjoy him.

I don't think we intend to relate to God this way. It's just easier to assimilate the concept that God is to be admired and reverenced. It's logical that we should serve him, pray to him, read about him, worship him, give to him. But enjoy him? Live life with him? That's harder to grasp.

Jesus addressed this issue in John, chapter 15, verses 1–10. Notice how many times the word *abide* is used.

I am the true vine, and My Father is the vinedresser. Every branch in Me that does not bear fruit He takes away; and every branch that bears fruit He prunes, that it may bear more fruit. You are already clean because of the word which I have spoken to you. *Abide* in Me, and I in you. As the branch cannot bear fruit of itself, unless it *abides* in the vine, neither can you, unless you *abide* in Me.

I am the vine, you are the branches. He who *abides* in Me, and I in him, bears much fruit; for without Me you can do nothing. If anyone does not *abide* in Me, he is cast out as a branch and is withered; and they gather them and throw them into the fire, and they are burned. If you *abide* in Me, and My words *abide* in you, you will ask what you desire, and it shall be done for you. By this My Father is glorified, that you bear much fruit; so you will be My disciples.

As the Father loved Me, I also have loved you; *abide* in My love. If you keep My commandments, you will *abide* in My love, just as I have kept My Father's commandments and *abide* in His love. (emphasis added)

As I mentioned, the term *abide* is repeated throughout this passage. It seems to be the theme here.

Abide means to live, remain, stay, continue, or dwell. It emphasizes the idea of long-term relationship. To abide in a particular place is to live there, not just to visit once in a while or to admire from a distance. Basically it means you can walk on the carpet and sit on the furniture without fear of maternal wrath.

Jesus tells us to abide in him and to abide in his love. Then he connects our abiding with things like joy, fruitfulness, obedience, and loving others.

If we don't understand what it means to abide in Jesus— that is, if we don't know how to live with him and enjoy him—we tend to jump over the *abide* part and just focus on how we can get the rest of the equation—the joy, the fruit, and the good works. That doesn't work too well, because abiding in Jesus is the key to all those things.

Now look at Psalm 51. Verse 12 says, "Restore to me the joy of Your salvation, and uphold me by Your generous Spirit." King David wrote this little verse. He wrote it shortly after he slept with his neighbor's wife and then killed her husband to cover up the adultery. Definitely not a highlight of his life. Now he was repenting and asking for restoration.

David clearly understood, centuries before Jesus died on the cross, that joy is a major element of salvation. He was saying, "I need some restoration work. I need this joy to be restored."

I find that many people don't know how to enjoy God. Sometimes they don't know if they should. They don't know if it's allowed or proper. It seems kind of irreverent. Other times they genuinely don't know how to enjoy God. They want to, but practically they don't understand how to just hang out with God.

A lot of us treat God like an expensive, antique piece of furniture. Have you ever gone over to a friend's house, and you see an old, beat-up chair, and you naturally assume it is meant for sitting? You start to sit down, and they're like, "Whoa, whoa, whoa! *Whoa!* What are you doing?"

"Um, sorry? I was going to sit here, on this sitting device."

"It's not for sitting."

"It's a chair."

"But it's not for sitting.

"Oh, of course. Why would it be? My bad."

"It's for admiring. It's expensive and old and cool."

Sometimes we treat God like an antique chair, when, in fact, God is a lot more like an IKEA couch. I don't mean in his worth or his beauty or his grandeur, of course—in every category he is beyond compare. But in terms of relationship, we often treat God more like an expensive antique, when he invites us to treat him like an IKEA couch.

Come on; we've all had one. It cost, like, eight dollars, right? And it's dark green for a reason. Dark green hides everything. And when the kids want to eat on the expensive couch, we say, "Don't eat on my couch. Go eat on your couch. It's already filled with all kinds of mysteries and treasures underneath those cushions. Go enjoy your IKEA couch."

Where do you really, truly do life? On the IKEA couch.

Or maybe you have one of those old recliners. It's a La-Z-Boy from the 1980s. Your wife and your kids have begged you to get rid of it. It smells, and it has your bodily impressions on it. Even when you're gone, it's like you're still sitting on it. If we wanted to buy you pants, we could get your size right there. But it's your happy place. You're having a tough workweek, it's Friday afternoon, you've got three hours left till you go home, and what's your motivating force? That chair. It's where you relax. It's where you live.

God wants to be lived in. God wants to be lived with. God wants you to recline on him.

Life with God is a loving relationship. It's not a job description or a business deal. It's not a school assignment or a sports contract. We can't reduce it to a list of dos and don'ts.

We just experience him. We grow closer to him. We learn to be aware of his presence, to appreciate his companionship, to share the joy he feels about our lives.

Enjoying life and enjoying God are inextricably connected. We enjoy life the most when we enjoy God; and when we enjoy God, we love life even more. Life is good, and with God it's even better.

Enjoying God doesn't mean moving to the mountains and spending every minute in solitary prayer. We can enjoy God in prayer and worship and solitude, of course, but enjoying God is much more than that. It means being aware that God is with us and for us—everywhere, all the time, no matter what. It means learning from him and leaning on him. It means developing a real relationship with him.

What if, today, God wants to laugh with you for a few minutes? What if he wants to cry with you? What if he wants to go on a hike with you, or talk with you in the kitchen, or go on break with you at work, or do study hall with you at school? Can you imagine what that would look like?

I'm not talking about something spooky or esoteric or weird. I'm talking about opening our minds and hearts to the reality of God's presence.

We don't have to do life alone. We were never meant to be alone. We can experience life with the author of life—the one who designed us, the one who knows us better than we do ourselves. That's when life really becomes enjoyable.

God makes life more fun. God makes life make sense. God makes life worth living.

Frosted-Glass People

I love this phrase out of John, chapter 15: "As the Father loved Me, I also have loved you" (v. 9). That's incredible. The exact same love that God has for Jesus, Jesus has for us. It's not hard to imagine God loving Jesus; Jesus was perfect. Jesus loved everyone. Jesus did everything God wanted.

But sometimes we think, *How could Jesus love me like that?*

I've never done that much for him. Actually, I mess up regularly. There's no way Jesus loves me like God loves Jesus.

I'm convinced that one of the greatest hindrances to enjoying God is something the Bible refers to as condemnation.

Let me illustrate. I do a fair bit of air travel, so I've also spent a lot of time in purgatory—I mean airports. I've found that when you are in airports often and for long periods of time, having a quiet place to rest or get away can make all the difference.

Now, as anyone who flies a lot knows, if you fly enough with a particular airline, eventually they'll give you some level of membership status. This status proves that you fly a lot and that you have no life.

For some reason, this status is usually named after precious metals or rare gems. "Congratulations! You're now a gold member," or "You've been promoted to diamond status."

I've figured out you don't want to get into any lesser materials. If you move from gold to silver to wood to clay, that's not good. You want to stay on the precious, rare side of metals and gems. That's key.

A couple of airlines have given me this kind of status, which I appreciate. Recently I was at an airport and arrived at that secret hideaway, that special lounge. At the front desk was a nice lady who was going to check my credentials and see if in fact I'd spent enough time with this airline to allow me to go behind the frosted glass, where the happy people are, people who are enjoying scones, and dates with cheese lodged in them, and mozzarella chunks, and sparkling mineral water, and free coffee. This is where you want to be. Overstuffed chairs, hyperfast Wi-Fi—you want to be with the frosted-glass people. Trust me. You don't want to be out roaming purgatory.

Typically what happens is you give them your card and say, "Here, I have no life, check for yourself."

And they are like, "Wow, you spend your entire life in a tube in the air."

Then they swipe it, and they usually stare mysteriously at the screen for a moment, and then they type a little bit, and then they go, "Welcome, Mr. Smith." And you get to go back with the frosted-glass people.

But once in a while, if you haven't been flying as frequently as you normally do, you will come to the front desk, and they will swipe your card, pause, type, pause, call one of their coworkers over, look uncomfortable, and type some more.

Typically while this is going on, a long line of precious metals and rare gems is forming behind you. All the gold, silver, diamond, and platinum people are persistently trying to press their way behind the frosted glass, and you are the hindrance.

And now you have the coworker, the manager, and the owner of the airline all crowded around the front desk, looking worriedly at the screen. And finally one of them says, "Sir, we're sorry."

You're thinking, *Sorry for what?*

"Sir, your status has changed. There's no easy way to say this, but you are no longer gold. You are silver. Actually—correction—you are, in fact, copper now. Your status is plummeting as we speak. You will now be escorted off the premises. Have a nice day."

While you're walking out, diamond and gold people are like, "I don't even want you in my periphery, you piece of clay."

The hardest part is you were already there. You saw over the frosted glass. But you were rejected. It would be nice—just speaking to the airlines for a moment—if you could somehow tell us our status has changed privately. Give us some dignity. It's kind of embarrassing in front of all the gems and precious metals.

This makes for a great example of how a lot of people view their relationship with God. We think if we don't do enough, if we don't perform well enough, or if we do too much of the wrong thing, God will, without warning and at the most embarrassing time, change our status. "Sorry. You no longer have the access you once had. You cannot expect the resources you once had. You cannot expect the blessing that you once experienced. Your status has changed."

We don't verbalize that thought so blatantly and candidly, but our actions and our prayers and our emotions reveal it is there, deep inside. We think that based on our performance, our status before God is subject to change.

One of my favorite passages in the entire Bible is found in Romans, chapter 8, verses 1–4:

So now there is no condemnation for those who belong to Christ Jesus. And because you belong to him, the power of the life-giving Spirit has freed you from the power of sin that leads to death. The law of Moses was unable to save us because of the weakness of our sinful nature. So God did what the law could not do. He sent his own Son in a body like the bodies we sinners have. And in that body God declared an end to sin's control over us by giving his Son as a sacrifice for our sins. He did this so that the just requirement of the law would be fully satisfied for us, who no longer follow our sinful nature but instead follow the Spirit. (NLT)

That word *condemnation* means a guilty verdict. This passage emphatically contradicts the notion that our status before God can change. It declares without hesitation, qualification, exception, or apology that if we belong to Jesus, we cannot be condemned. We cannot be declared guilty or sentenced for our sins.

If we follow Jesus, our status before God is righteous. The gavel has come down and our righteousness is secure in the work of Jesus Christ. God's verdict is not subject to change based on our performance. We didn't become righteous because of our performance, and we can't lose our righteousness because of our performance. We don't have to worry about getting escorted off God's premises. We have access, we have resources, and we have blessings because of Jesus.

It is easy to hear this sort of message and get excited about it. We hear a preacher talking about God's forgiveness and grace on Sunday, and we're like, "Woohoo! I'm in! This is great!"

But then Monday comes around, and it's really hard to apply this reality when we're having one of those moments when we lose our minds, or make dumb decisions, or go off on somebody, or do that stupid, ridiculous thing we swore we'd never do again.

Suddenly, here comes the negative emotion. Here come the bad feelings. Here comes that sense that our status cannot possibly be the same as it was in church yesterday. That's what the Bible calls condemnation. It's a very real phenomenon.

If you are a follower of Jesus, a Christian, and have never experienced condemnation, you might be God. For the rest of us mortals, we've all experienced it. Guilt. Shame. A sense that our status has changed.

I'm going to take this a step further. This might sound weird at first, but I think we actually, in a very sadistic way, enjoy condemnation. Why? Because condemnation is logical; and in a weird, twisted, dark sense, it gratifies our flesh. It actually feels right to feel horrible, to feel depressed, to feel dejected, to feel despair. "I messed up. I did something so stupid. This serves me right."

But in fact, condemnation doesn't serve us at all. In the verses above, the Bible says that condemnation should have no part in our existence on this planet if we belong to Jesus.

As humans, we are experts at confusing our feelings with reality. We take our negative emotions and thoughts at face value, and we think, *I feel bad, so I must be bad. I feel guilty, so I must be guilty. And if I'm disappointed and mad at myself, God must be way more disappointed and mad at me.*

Since we feel condemned, we think we are condemned. And since we think we are condemned, we work harder to regain our lost status. Instead of going confidently to God and asking for his grace to get back up and move forward in life, we try to patch ourselves up and put ourselves back together so we can attain the status of righteous before God again.

Ironically, since we will never measure up to perfection, the more we try to earn our righteousness, the worse we feel. It's the cycle of condemnation.

I find it's far easier to believe we are sinners than to believe we are righteous. But we are already righteous through Jesus. It's a gift, and it's called grace. How much time do we waste as Jesus followers trying to recover what we have had all along?

Party Like a Prodigal

I'll end with one of the most well-known parables Jesus ever told. It's usually referred to as the parable of the prodigal son, and it's found in Luke, chapter 15.

A father has two sons. One day the younger son says, "Dad, I want my inheritance right now." His dad gives it to him, and the son moves to some wild city, lives a crazy lifestyle, and wastes all the money. Eventually he's starving, he's a mess, and he's desperate, so he takes a job working on a pig farm. At some point, it strikes him that he's literally jealous of the scraps the pigs are eating. At that moment he comes to his senses and thinks, *I'm going back to Dad's house, and I'm going to ask him for a job. I know I can't be his son, but at least I won't starve. I'll earn my keep.*

So he prepares a pathetic little speech, and he makes his

way to Dad's house. The Bible says, "But when he was still a great way off, his father saw him and had compassion, and ran and fell on his neck and kissed him."

The son launches into his prepared speech: "I have sinned against heaven and in your sight, and am no longer worthy to be called your son."

Dad completely ignores what his son just said, then turns to his servants. "Bring out the best robe and put it on him, and put a ring on his hand and sandals on his feet. And bring the fatted calf here and kill it, and let us eat and be merry; for this my son was dead and is alive again; he was lost and is found."

And the Bible says they "began to be merry." Translation: they partied, and they partied hard.

I wonder how much time had elapsed between when the son returned and when he was doing the Electric Slide on the dance floor? A few minutes? A couple of hours?

It couldn't have been too long, because the older brother has been out in the field, working and sweating and toiling, and when he returns home, the party is in full swing. Before he even gets to the house, he can hear music and laughter wafting across the fields.

It's hard for me to wrap my brain around this illogical, ridiculous, scandalous scene that Jesus is describing. And remember, the whole point of the story is that the father's love for the prodigal son is an illustration of God's love for us.

The boy has wasted the hard-earned money of his father. He has dishonored him and disobeyed him. He has lived wildly and ridiculously. He's barely been home long enough to shower, shave, and put on his new outfit and jewelry, and now this wayward, AWOL son is on a dance floor with his cronies.

What?

The only person in the story who is thinking logically is the older son. He's like, "Dad, this doesn't make any sense. My brother is an idiot, but you hired a DJ and threw him a party."

Most of us, if we were throwing the party, would tell the younger boy, "Son, you sit over there. Don't even think about dancing. You sit there and watch everyone else have fun, and you think about the stupid thing you did with my money." But not this father. Think about that. He insisted that his boy dance. He insisted that he celebrate his own return.

Here's the principle Jesus was communicating: When we sin, the most powerful place we can be is enjoying his love. It's not sulking in a corner, it's not beating ourselves up over our mistakes, and it's not making a lot of empty vows. It's reveling and rejoicing in the never-ending righteousness of God.

We need the joy of our salvation most when we feel like we deserve it the least.

14

A Whole New World

Aladdin

I'm a big fan of Disney's animated movies, or at least of most of them. I don't know what it is, but the songs get stuck in my head. There is a Disney song for every situation you encounter in life. Some people quote *The Godfather*. Some quote *Monty Python and the Holy Grail*. I quote Walt Disney. Those are the true classics.

Do you remember *Aladdin*? It came out longer ago than I care to think about, but I remember it clearly. I still find myself singing "A Whole New World" at the top of my lungs every once in a while: "A whole new world / A new fantastic point of view . . ."

Technically, the song was referring to the romantic view from atop a flying floor mat, but I'm going to apply it to the new life we discover in Jesus. Like I said, Disney has a song for everything.

The Bible says in 2 Corinthians, chapter 5, "Therefore, if anyone is in Christ, he is a new creation; old things have passed away; behold, all things have become new" (v. 17). This verse doesn't say we will get a new start, or a new opportunity, or a few improvements, or some fantastic additions. It says that through Jesus we are new creations. Everything about our lives is new.

I'm convinced that God wants to show us a whole new world. I'm not talking about heaven, either, although that is the ultimate and greatest new world. I'm talking about a new way to live here on earth.

I believe Jesus came to earth first and foremost to pay the penalty for our sins, but I believe he also came to model for us how to live life the way it was meant to be. If we are willing to listen and learn, he shows us how to find the satisfaction and fulfillment God intends for us.

This new path to satisfaction, this whole new world, is not found in striving and working and forcing, but in enjoying God.

Most Valuable Passenger

I'm going to share another airline story. This is therapeutic for me. I hope it is for you too.

I have particular problems with boarding airplanes. The game has changed a bit lately, because you used to check all your luggage. Now nobody wants to check anything, so they cram two weeks' worth of clothes into the biggest carry-on they can find. It weighs eighty pounds and it's so full they had to duct-tape it shut, but at least they don't have to pay a fee, and they know the airline isn't going to lose their stuff.

So you have two hundred people in a crowded waiting room, and they all have their oversized carry-ons and purses and briefcases and musical instruments and pets and small children. And we've all done this before, so we know one thing for sure: there isn't going to be enough overhead space to go around.

As soon as the airline employee at the counter starts to talk into the mic, the whole room rushes forward. The airline hasn't even started the boarding process yet, but that doesn't stop everyone from crowding around the gate, jockeying for position and waiting for their zone to board.

My favorite is when the airline people get on the microphone to comfort us. "Everyone will get on the plane. Calm down. Stand back. Make room." That just makes us more nervous and desperate. We suspect we are being lied to.

As I mentioned before, I fly pretty regularly, so one particular airline has given me what they call MVP status. I don't really know what the P stands for: Most Valuable Passenger, maybe? Anyway, as a perk, I'm supposed to be given early access to boarding the plane.

I don't do really close crowds like that. I don't do herds or stampedes well. Maybe crowding doesn't bother you, but I have personal space issues. All I can think is, *I'm breathing what they're releasing.* Not a good situation. So rather than squeeze into the mass of humanity piled at the gate, I hang back until boarding actually begins.

As a pastor I believe that all humans are of equal value. You believe that, too, I'm sure. The problem is, it doesn't seem that way when they say, "We'd like to begin boarding with our super-special, better-than-you MVPs." I have to finagle and wiggle my way through two hundred people to get to the front, and it doesn't feel very pastoral to step over pets and small children and walk past all those desperate, pleading faces. But I need space for my carry-on, too, so I press on.

I don't know how to do this gracefully. "Um, are you—are you MVP? Are you valuable? No? Oh, well, I am. Excuse me, I'll just be cutting through here." Worst of all is when one of the faces recognizes me. "Pastor Judah? Is that you? Are you in first class?" There's no elegant way to handle this, because when you're boarding, it's every man for himself. It's mayhem.

There is something desperate about competing with a mass of humanity for limited resources. This feeling isn't limited to airport gates, of course—for many of us, it seems to be a regular part of life.

There's a story in the fifth chapter of John, verses 1–15, that illustrates this struggle.

> After this there was a feast of the Jews, and Jesus went up to Jerusalem. Now there is in Jerusalem by the Sheep Gate a pool, which is called in Hebrew, Bethesda, having five porches. In these lay a great multitude of sick people, blind, lame, paralyzed, waiting for the moving of the water. For an angel went down at a certain time into the pool and stirred

up the water; then whoever stepped in first, after the stirring of the water, was made well of whatever disease he had. Now a certain man was there who had an infirmity thirty-eight years. When Jesus saw him lying there, and knew that he already had been in that condition a long time, He said to him, "Do you want to be made well?"

The sick man answered Him, "Sir, I have no man to put me into the pool when the water is stirred up; but while I am coming, another steps down before me."

Jesus said to him, "Rise, take up your bed and walk." And immediately the man was made well, took up his bed, and walked.

And that day was the Sabbath. The Jews therefore said to him who was cured, "It is the Sabbath; it is not lawful for you to carry your bed."

He answered them, "He who made me well said to me, 'Take up your bed and walk.'"

Then they asked him, "Who is the Man who said to you, 'Take up your bed and walk'?" But the one who was healed did not know who it was, for Jesus had withdrawn, a multitude being in that place. Afterward Jesus found him in the temple, and said to him, "See, you have been made well. Sin no more, lest a worse thing come upon you."

The man departed and told the Jews that it was Jesus who had made him well.

What's funny to me is that we read ancient biblical passages like this and we idealize the situation. We imagine orderly rows of people lounging poolside and sipping cool drinks. And when the angel stirs the beautiful, crystal clear waters, all the lame and paralyzed and blind people look at each other and say, "Go ahead, you were here first." And one at a time, they are all healed.

No, it's more like boarding an airplane at Christmas, after the flight has been delayed for six hours. It is chaos. It is every man for himself.

Can you imagine the tension by that pool? The story says there are "great multitudes" of people there. How many is that? Safe to say, we are talking hundreds of desperate, hurting people. And every last one is thinking, *Maybe this will be my time to get healed.*

It is a dog-eat-dog environment. It is a culture of chaos and disorder and stress and tension and anxiety. Everyone is trying to take advantage of and beat other people who are also in need.

If you step back for a moment from this passage, you realize this man is representative of you and me, and this culture is representative of humanity. Our society is often sick and desperate. Our relationships are often fractured and self-serving. We often find ourselves surrounded by tension, posturing, manipulation. We feel like we have to join in to get ahead, just to survive. We don't want to function this way, but there seems to be no other option.

The relational and social and emotional issues are real. This pool scenario is our planet and the people on it. We are that man.

Get Up

Jesus asks the man by the pool, "Do you want to be made well?"

The obvious answer would have been "Yes! Of course! Are you kidding me?" But the man points to his impossible situation. He's been sick for nearly four decades. He has no one to help him get ahead in life. He's had a lot of almost successes. But someone always beats him to the healing. Someone is always faster or smarter or more ruthless.

Doesn't that sound like life on this planet? Have you ever felt like this? You're on the verge of a great business deal and the rug gets pulled out from under you. Someone comes in and gets the deal and prospers, and your family is left on the edge of bankruptcy.

Maybe you keep replaying in your mind those moments when you were right there on the edge of the pool, on the edge of getting what you'd dreamed about for years. But someone else was always quicker or smoother or more educated or more ruthless. And you are tempted to conclude that life belongs to the fastest, the smoothest, the most stubborn, the best manipulators and networkers, and the people who use others to work their way to the pool of their dreams. Maybe that's the only way to get ahead in this life.

Many of us live with incredible tension and anxiety because we think that our dreams will come true if we just get the right degree, if we just meet the right people, if we just get the right job. We assume our happiness is tied to our success, and our success depends on our performance. So we sweat and struggle and scheme and strategize, and we wonder why we aren't enjoying life.

"Do you want to be made well?" Jesus asks the man.

"I've tried, but—"

"Get up. Right now. Pick up your mat, and walk away free and healed and happy."

The fulfillment of this man's dreams is not found in jockeying his way to the top. It's not found in pushing his way to the front. It is found in Jesus.

You have to wonder what this man is thinking when Jesus tells him to get up. *Get up? Sure. Easy for you to say. I've tried to get up for years.*

Have you ever felt that way? Someone tells you that God wants to help you, and you're thinking, *It can't be that easy. You know how many years I've tried to improve myself? You know how many years I've tried to go after my dreams? You can't tell me just to get up. You can't tell me just to believe in Jesus.*

The man gets up. How—and why—does this man respond? Does he feel something in his body? Does he feel compelled internally, inexplicably? Whatever the reason, he simply gets up. And now he's doing something he has only dreamed about doing his whole life. It happened in one moment, after one simple, illogical invitation by this mysterious man.

I think this man realizes that he has no other choice. His way isn't working and never will. He is at the end of himself. And then he meets Jesus.

Are you at the end of yourself? Are you tired of the rat race and the mayhem you think you have to endure to find true happiness? Jesus offers another way.

Holy Party Poopers

What gets really crazy here is how people respond. They've seen this guy for thirty-eight years. They know his plight. They know they could have never helped him themselves.

But what is remarkable and even overwhelming is that because these people are so fixated on the law, they can't celebrate the fact that this man is now standing and walking. All they can see is that someone healed him on the Sabbath, and now he is carrying his bed on the Sabbath. They had defined these things as work, and so the law is being broken. That's all they care about. Instead of congratulating him, they tell him to put down his bed, and they start interrogating him about the incident to find out how the crime began.

I wish I could jump into the narrative and say, "Can we all stop for a moment and remember this guy hasn't carried anything for thirty-eight years? Carrying his bed is cause for celebration, people. Let's talk about the law later. Right now, let's just have at least a nanosecond-long party, because this man is standing and walking and carrying. Is that breaking the law? I don't know. But what is really important right now is that God is at work in him."

Let me ask this, though. Have you ever been one of those critics? I have. God might be doing a miracle in people's hearts, but because their exterior has not caught up with what I think God-followers should look and act and talk like, I get bent out of shape. I don't notice that they are being healed, restored, and saved. All I notice is they are not adhering to the lifestyle I think they should adhere to.

"Those people know Jesus? Really? Well, how come they are doing this or that?"

Maybe we don't realize it, but they are carrying their beds. In other words, they are currently, right now, as we speak, and as we criticize, being set free from what was truly crippling them. We couldn't have done that for them, but Jesus did. And he did it in an instant. But sometimes all we see is that they are still doing things that make us uncomfortable. They don't look like us or talk like us, and we can't see past that and recognize that Jesus has saved their souls.

Might I suggest that we be slow to criticize and critique and quick to celebrate what God is doing in people's lives? That we focus less on the little things and more on the fact that people are knowing and enjoying God?

Just a thought.

How to Stop Sinning

The story goes on. Everyone is like, "Who told you to pick up your bed and walk?"

He has no idea. "Uh, I don't even know his name. Sorry. You know, he told me to get up, and I kind of just . . . got up.

Then he told me to carry my bed and head home. So I'm going to go ahead and do what the guy that healed me said and—no offense—ignore you guys."

What I love about this story, though, is that the man eventually learns Jesus' name. How? Jesus comes back and finds him.

This man isn't on the celebrity A-list or B-list or any other list. We don't even know his name. It is more than anyone could have expected for Jesus to go out of his way to heal him in the first place. But to seek him out a second time?

Jesus goes out of his way to say, "By the way, my name is Jesus." Why?

Because this wasn't as much about the healing as it was about the man himself. Jesus didn't just want the man to walk—he wanted the man to know him. He wanted the man to have a relationship with God, the source of all satisfaction and miracles and life. He wanted the man to enjoy God.

Then Jesus says, "Now here's the deal. You've got to stop sinning. Sin is the problem. Stop sinning or a worse thing will come upon you."

Sometimes we read this, and we think, *Okay, now that I know Jesus, I'd better not sin anymore. If I do, something bad will happen to me.*

But what Jesus is trying to do here is point the man beyond a physical healing to the spiritual healing he really needed. He is saying that illness is bad, but sin is worse.

The consequence of sin is eternal separation from God. The Bible calls it hell.

Jesus is saying that the man needed to look to him not just for a physical healing, great as that was, but for salvation from the real problem: sin. Jesus is saying, "You need me. Follow me. Sin will take you down an eternal path that you are not going to like. But I am the answer."

How do we stop sinning and suffering the consequences of sin? Not by trying harder, but simply by following the sinless Savior.

Sometimes we think life is about happiness, about satisfaction, and about living as pain-free as possible. God does desire our happiness, and much of Scripture is focused on helping us maximize our enjoyment and fulfillment in this life. But life is much bigger than the few decades we spend on this planet. God wants to be our God eternally. He wants to make us happy and fulfilled eternally. And the doorway to that new world is Jesus.

Unforced Rhythms of Grace

The last verse in this story shows the power of a changed life. The man who was healed goes everywhere telling everyone about Jesus. He understands. He gets it. The story isn't about the healing—it's about the Healer. The man has moved from the stressful, tense, every-man-for-himself environment to a place of freedom. He has entered a new world order, a new way of doing life. Instead of using people, he just wants to share with them what he has discovered.

Do you see how drastic the change is when Jesus comes into your life? This is not a renovation or a remodel. It's not an upgrade, an addition, or an accessory. This is a new creation. This is a new world. This is a new system.

"Behold, all things have become new" (2 Corinthians 5:17). The new world order introduced by the death, burial, resurrection, and ascension of Jesus Christ trumps our social constructs and our ways of operating. It overflows out of our personal lives and brings life to our friendships, our business dealings, our marriages, our parenting, our decisions.

Jesus says in Matthew, chapter 11, verses 28–30: "Are you tired? Worn out? Burned out on religion? Come to me. Get away with me and you'll recover your life. I'll show you how to take a real rest. Walk with me and work with me—watch how I do it. Learn the unforced rhythms of grace. I won't lay anything heavy or ill-fitting on you. Keep company with me and you'll learn to live freely and lightly" (MSG).

Are you tired of the mayhem around the pool, of the struggle to survive and conquer in a hostile environment, of trying to do things your way, in your strength, with your resources?

"Come to me," Jesus says. "Get away with me and you'll recover your life. I'll show you how to take a real rest."

Learn his "unforced rhythms of grace," as this passage so beautifully puts it. Learn to wait on him and lean into him. Learn to enjoy him even when—*especially* when—you don't know how to solve the problems you face.

Jesus will show you a whole new world.

15

True Satisfaction

Three Pounds Full

In the last chapter, I picked on people who cram two weeks' worth of clothing into one bag. I admit, I have firsthand experience with this. I am the quintessential overpacker. When I go on a trip, I like to keep my wardrobe options open. So it can get a little challenging getting all the clothes I might want to wear into one little suitcase—or three. First-world problems, I know.

I usually end up engaging the weight of my entire body to cram and compress the clothes into the bag. My knees are on the bag and I'm bouncing up and down trying to close the suitcase. The zipper is complaining and crying out to God for mercy. Eventually I win, and the bag is officially packed.

But then I get to the airport, and naturally the bag weighs three pounds too much. Chelsea told me I should check before I left, but I didn't. And the airline attendant says, "Sir, you'll have to move those three pounds into another bag."

And I'm like, "It's three pounds. My five-year-old can lift three pounds. Would you like her to help you lift it?" Just kidding, that would be rude. I say, "Yes, ma'am."

I start to unzip the bag, and of course everyone in line is watching because they have nothing better to do than watch poor souls repack their personal items in public. And I know what they are thinking: *He's a dude and he packs more clothes than my wife and three daughters combined.*

I slide the zipper, and at some point everything inside bursts out like a jack-in-the-box. And naturally, my Spanx are on top. I move the three pounds to another bag, and repeat the process of cramming and stuffing and jamming so I can close the zipper. Definitely a great way to start a trip.

What I do to my suitcases—cram, jam, overflow, stuff, fill—illustrates what Jesus does for our lives. He fills us, he completes us, and he satisfies us beyond what we could ask or even imagine.

Do you remember when we looked at the Sermon on the Mount in chapter 12? Jesus said, "Do not think that I came to destroy the Law or the Prophets. I did not come to destroy but to fulfill" (Matthew 5:17). The original Greek word translated *fulfill* means "to fill completely." Jesus is saying that he came to satisfy and fulfill and complete everything the Bible says.

Based on what the Bible says about Jesus, I would take this a step further. Jesus didn't come just to satisfy the law and fulfill the Scripture. He came to satisfy and complete and fill humanity. That is who he is: a fulfiller, a completer.

John records a definitive statement by Jesus in the Gospel

of John, chapter 10. "The thief's purpose is to steal and kill and destroy. My purpose is to give them a rich and satisfying life" (v. 10 NLT). In other words, fulfilling the needs and desires and hopes of mankind is the nature of his mission to humanity. He came to make our lives complete. He came to give us true life.

We are all looking for a sense of value and purpose. We have a deep, driving, and even desperate need for true satisfaction. We tend to look for it in things like pleasure, power, wealth, fame, or work. There is nothing wrong with those things, but by themselves, they can't bring us lasting fulfillment. We won't find what we're looking for until we find Jesus.

Scripture reveals a God who desires to completely satisfy, stuff, jam, and cram our souls with satisfaction and fulfillment.

Chore Chart

This satisfied life is found in God, as I've mentioned throughout this book. The problem, though, is that we still attempt to relate to God based on our efforts, our merit, and our terms. That never works.

When my older sister and I were growing up, my mom and dad tried valiantly to get us to do chores. I say "tried" because their efforts were remarkably unsuccessful. My mom estimates she and Dad created twelve different chore charts to encourage and motivate and obligate us to do chores. Twelve. Imagine that. Twelve different charts were produced to try to get two offspring to do something productive in their childhood.

My dad was very creative and innovative, and he loved to design the charts. We had stick-on stars for one chart, and little stamps for another, and so on. He liked creating the charts more than enforcing them, and that was part of the problem. The charts were always creative and colorful and basically unreadable, but they were still awesome.

I remember these chore charts would go on the refrigerator or on some wall, and every day we were supposed to check the chart and do what it said. There were usually four or five chores per day, and I would start out pretty good. I'd do my first chore, then my second chore. Then I'd be like, "Look at the time! Who has time for three more chores?" If you have any kids or know any kids or ever were a kid, you'll understand. "Chores? Ain't nobody got time for that." So the chore charts usually lasted about half a day for me.

When I bailed on the chore chart, my dad would say, "Son, either you do your chores or I'm going to spank you." And I'd say, "I'll take the spanking." I knew that it would be three or four swats, and then it would be over. The chores would take me a solid three or four hours. I was happy about the spanking. And Dad was helpless.

But my parents' noble effort to get their two children to do chores based on a chore chart is a wonderful example of human nature. Charts and rules work to a certain extent, but they have no power to create inner motivation. They have no power to change us.

Before I continue, I understand there are anomalies out there. My wife is one of them. She's just wired that way. She loves to-do lists. She loves to know the expectations and rules and requirements. She wants to get the star and the prize at the end.

But in general, chore charts and rule books are merely external tools to help control our behavior. They don't change us, they don't motivate us, and they don't produce any sort of relationship with the rule maker.

Meet the Bachelor

Fifteen hundred years before Jesus was born, God created the first chore chart. It was a ten-part list that we call the Ten Commandments. God wrote out the chores on stone tablets and gave them to Moses.

During all the centuries before Jesus, millions attempted to fulfill this chore chart, but no one could. Not one. Ultimately, of course, God didn't want Israel or the rest of the world to relate to him based on a chore chart. It was a temporary system put in place to help lead people to Jesus.

This leads us to Mark, chapter 10. Here, the Bible describes an interesting exchange—ultimately a tragic, sorrowful exchange— between Jesus and a successful young businessman.

> Now as He was going out on the road, one came running, knelt before Him, and asked Him, "Good Teacher, what shall I do that I may inherit eternal life?"

So Jesus said to him, "Why do you call Me good? No one is good but One, that is, God. You know the commandments: 'Do not commit adultery,' 'Do not murder,' 'Do not steal,' 'Do not bear false witness,' 'Do not defraud,' 'Honor your father and your mother.' "

And he answered and said to Him, "Teacher, all these things I have kept from my youth."

Then Jesus, looking at him, loved him, and said to him, "One thing you lack: Go your way, sell whatever you have and give to the poor, and you will have treasure in heaven; and come, take up the cross, and follow Me."

But he was sad at this word, and went away sorrowful, for he had great possessions.

Then Jesus looked around and said to His disciples, "How hard it is for those who have riches to enter the kingdom of God!" And the disciples were astonished at His words. But Jesus answered again and said to them, "Children, how hard it is for those who trust in riches to enter the kingdom of God! It is easier for a camel to go through the eye of a needle than for a rich man to enter the kingdom of God."

And they were greatly astonished, saying among themselves, "Who then can be saved?"

But Jesus looked at them and said, "With men it is impossible, but not with God; for with God all things are possible." (verses 17–27)

We don't know the man's name, but if we look at the story here as well as in Matthew and Luke, we find the

Bible describes him as rich, as young, and as a ruler. He had a lot going for him in terms of what this world values: youth, strength, vitality, influence, wealth, authority. Besides that, he seems to be just a great guy. He is concerned with his morality and his spirituality and with following the rules. He's ambitious. He has his life together. He's a shining beacon of success. Basically he's the ultimate bachelor.

But he's still looking for something. I think he knows, deep inside, that there is more to life than money and power and good deeds.

He has come to the right person for help. But he's asking the wrong questions.

Ten Minus Six Is One

Something about Jesus gets his attention, and he comes running to find out the secret to the happiness and peace that Jesus has. He says, "Good Teacher."

Instantly, Jesus addresses this. "You call me good? No one's good except God." Jesus is gently reminding the young man that no human is good. The man clearly thinks pretty highly of himself, as we see later on when he assures Jesus he has kept all the commandments since he was a kid. So Jesus is reminding him that people are not inherently good.

Jesus wants this young man to realize from the outset that he needs to be looking beyond himself if he wants to find true life.

When Jesus tells the young man that no human being is good, he is also reminding the man that his statement implies Jesus is God. That's a key point. The man knows no one is good, yet he calls Jesus good. He must understand there is something different, something divine, about Jesus. And yet, instead of asking for relationship, he is asking for more rules. "What should I do to inherit eternal life?"

So Jesus humors him. "You've heard of the Ten Commandments, right? Do not commit adultery, do not murder . . ."

Jesus gets through six of them before the guy interrupts. "Yeah, yeah, yeah. I've got those. I've got all those."

That's probably a slight exaggeration. As I said, this guy likes himself. A lot.

Keep in mind that Jesus, as we saw earlier, is the fulfiller of the Law and the Prophets. That includes the Ten Commandments. So why is he bringing them up now? Is Jesus saying you have to fulfill the Ten Commandments if you want to get into heaven? That's bad news, because again, for a millennium and a half, millions of people have been trying that, and no one has done it.

No, it's a setup. Jesus has only mentioned six of the commandments before the zealous young man cuts him off. But then he says, "One thing you lack."

Hang on. Based on my calculations, Jesus quoted six out of ten, which leaves four. Right? Is my math correct? I know I had to take pre-algebra for three years, but I'm pretty sure I can handle ten minus six. I count four things lacking.

"One thing you lack."

What is Jesus doing? How can he say that? This seems unlawful and illegal. This is not consistent with the chore chart.

Jesus is telling the young man that it's not about a chore chart at all. God doesn't just want the man's conduct or actions or habits. He wants all of him. He wants relationship.

"There's only one thing you lack: give me everything."

"Huh?"

"Yeah. Scrap the steps and the components and the elements and the keys to success. Stop the empty pursuit of happiness, and follow me. I want you and me to be together forever. I'll show you true life."

Jesus isn't saying we should get rid of all our material possessions in order to be happy and go to heaven. Just a few verses later, Peter says, "Jesus, we've left everything for you."

And Jesus replies, "I know you have. You left your parents and possessions and everything, but you're going to receive a hundredfold in this life—friends, family, relationships, houses, and lands—and on top of that, you're going to have eternal life."

So Jesus is not telling this young man, "I hate stuff in general. I hate all material things. You need to get rid of everything. You need to be poor and broke and pretend like you're happy."

He's saying that there is just one thing the man needed to do, and it's the same thing we all need to do: trust Jesus with everything. He isn't saying you can't have money in the bank, but he's saying that the money in the bank shouldn't matter in comparison to him.

Happiness Is a Person

My favorite part of this story is this little phrase in the middle: "Then Jesus, looking at him, loved him." This wasn't law at work—this was love. Sometimes we love rules and laws and chore charts because they seem so tangible, so sensible. But they will never love us back. What Jesus offers is love. Love fulfills the law. It supersedes the law. It accomplishes what the law could never do: it draws us close to God rather than creating distance from God.

Jesus' request was motivated by love. It wasn't meant to frustrate the man; it was meant to set him free. His misguided and self-centered approach toward life might have looked good on the outside, and it might have gained him a measure of success based on the world's criteria; but it wasn't making him happy. Jesus was offering him authentic satisfaction.

The man thinks he is just a couple of rules, a couple of keys, a couple of motivational speeches away from happiness. But happiness is standing right in front of him. Jesus is what this man is looking for.

Sometimes people who believe in God think religion is the key to satisfaction. I've done it too. We think being a Christian is about reading the Bible through every year, or about praying a certain number of minutes every morning, or about giving a certain percentage of our income to the church. I'm not criticizing those things, but they will not bring you lasting joy.

Jesus is standing before you, offering you abundant life in him. Don't ask him what else you need to do to gain it. It isn't found in doing anything. It is found in him, in relationship with him, in following him.

To follow and to have faith are synonymous in this sense. When Jesus says, "Follow me," he is saying, "Have faith in me. Be with me. Watch how I do life. Let's live the adventure. You want satisfaction? You won't find it in a chore chart. You won't find it in customs and traditions and rituals. You'll find it in me."

The rich young leader's response is the saddest part of the story. "Sorry. Uh, I gotta go." And he walks away, sorrowful and unsatisfied.

I like how *The Message* paraphrase renders Jesus' response: "Looking at His disciples, Jesus said, 'Do you have any idea how difficult it is for people who "have it all" to enter God's kingdom?'" Jesus isn't talking literally about people with a lot of money, but about people who, for whatever reason, feel like they have it all together.

The disciples can't believe what they are hearing. "Well, then, who can be saved?" They are just as impressed by the have-it-all-together appearance of this young man as everyone else. If this guy can't make it, they reasoned, no one else stands a chance.

Jesus' response is blunt. "No chance at all, if you think you can pull it off by yourself" (v. 27).

Without God, we have no chance. We will never be satisfied. We will never be fulfilled. We might have possessions and be rich and young and influential, but we will walk away sorrowful from life. We have no chance at all if we think we can pull it off alone, but we have every chance in the world if we let God do it.

One of the great paradoxes of life is that our souls finally find satisfaction when we give up before God. That is when we discover the buoyancy, and the fullness, and the life, and the peace, and the contentment that we long for.

16

You Complete Me

Cheetahs with Paint

My wife and my middle child are both puzzle people. I am not, so what I am about to share is secondhand information. I have no personal emotional investment in putting together puzzles.

Honestly, I don't understand why people would get enjoyment out of putting together the pieces of a picture when they already know what it's going to look like. Even worse, when they finish, they immediately tear it apart, box it up, and start on another one. I would be like, "Let's glue it together. Maybe frame it." But no; they are on to the next puzzle.

I have heard that the most frustrating thing for puzzle people is when they get to the end of the process and discover there is a piece missing. They've done all this work, put forth all this effort, and the puzzle is incomplete. It's imperfect. There is no closure or satisfaction or sense of accomplishment. I've heard this is very emotional for puzzle people. I wouldn't know.

Although I feel no emotional loss when a puzzle remains incomplete, there is another area of my life where I can understand the frustration with imperfection: I absolutely and unequivocally cannot stand to have stains on my clothes. Sometimes, for example, I panic because I think there is something on my shirt, only to discover it's a piece of colored fuzz. And I'm like, *Breathe. Breathe. It's not a big deal. You're fine. It wasn't real.* Ketchup, mustard, markers—these are my great enemies.

Call me crazy, but this is real for me. If I get a stain, no matter how small or faint, I'm done. I can't function. I will go find something else to wear, and I'll give whatever it was away because I won't ever use it again.

Recently I was subjected to maybe one of the worst experiences of my life, and it had to do with this particular paranoia. Our church has an annual summer kids' camp. We typically have team competitions, and during activity times, the teams are rewarded for their performance with kids' camp "cash." At the end of camp, the team with the most fake money wins. You can also get money by showing team spirit, by following rules, by being in the right place at the right time, by flattering staff members, and so on. It's basically totally subjective and unfair, but it's fun.

So at this camp, I was out in the activity field, and I was handing out kids' camp money. I was teaching the kids valuable moral lessons by throwing dollars in the air and watching them hurt each other to get them.

I came upon an activity station under the supervision— and I use the word *supervision* lightly—of two of my friends, Elijah and Annemarie. This station was the paint station, and the kids earned cash by soaking oversized sponges in neon paint and smashing them on their counselors.

Somehow, somebody thought this was would be a good idea, that this would be fun. I think it's beyond toleration. This is why I'm not a counselor. I don't want anyone to paint me. Ever.

So I was there, giving Annemarie and Elijah a hard time because I'm their pastor and that is one of my pastoral responsibilities. Then Annemarie did one of the darkest things she's ever done in her lifetime.

There were at least fifty of these fourth- and fifth-grade boys at the paint station. They were clearly hyped up on adrenaline, sleep deprivation, and orange Gatorade. And Annemarie pointed me out to the hungry pack. "You see that man? You see your pastor, Pastor Judah? I will give two hundred thousand camp dollars to the first person who can paint their handprint on him."

Instantly, kids' camp turned into the Discovery Channel, and I was the gazelle and they were the cheetahs. I was now running around the open field, trying to avoid what is, in fact, my worst nightmare.

As I mentioned before, I try to stay in good shape. But I can't compete with cheetahs. They were tireless, and they were motivated by team spirit and greed and Gatorade. The kids and their counselors caught up with me, and within seconds I was smeared and soiled and stained with neon evil.

So I did what any grown man would do. I threw stacks of money into the air as a distraction, and I sneaked away dejected, defeated, depressed. I walked directly to the campus office, shut the door, and sulked.

Then my mother, who was also at camp, heard what happened and came to console me. And I said to my mother, the person who raised me, the person whose passion for cleanliness and order probably contributed to my obsession: "Mom, I—I don't understand. Why, Mom? I can't do this."

My mother replied, and I quote: "Suck it up, son. You're a pastor."

She was right, of course. Neon paint stains and missing puzzle pieces are minor issues. But in a tiny, humorous way, they illustrate the emptiness and incompleteness that many people experience in their souls. We've probably all felt it to some degree: a nagging inner sense that something is missing or out of order, that we don't measure up, that we are incomplete.

A sense of incompleteness will dramatically affect how we do relationships. Our insecurities and emptiness define how we befriend people and relate to people and interact with people.

If we are insecure, we tend to use people instead of serving them. We tend to take from them instead of adding value to them because we are driven to satisfy our internal incompleteness. Relationships become all about fulfilling ourselves. And that just produces drama.

The first chapter of John's gospel, verses 14–17, says this:

And the Word [Jesus] became flesh and dwelt among us, and we beheld His glory, the glory as of the only begotten of the Father, full of grace and truth . . . And of His fullness we have all received, and grace for grace. For the law was given through Moses, but grace and truth came through Jesus Christ.

Notice the word *full*. John wrote that Jesus is full of grace and truth, and then he said that anyone can receive from his fullness.

Jesus is the first human being ever who is complete. He is full. He lacks nothing. He has no deficiency. He has no needs. I don't mean that he never had any physical and relational needs, of course. While he was walking this planet, the Bible shows him experiencing real needs, such as hunger, exhaustion, and loneliness.

But internally, Jesus was full. He was secure and complete. He didn't have the kind of emotional baggage that most of us carry around. He didn't have a nagging, gnawing sense of not measuring up. He didn't wonder if he was good enough or popular enough or smart enough. He didn't need relationships to reassure himself that he was valuable or important. Jesus was complete. Jesus was full.

Ultimately, God is the answer to our emptiness. He created humanity, and until we are in a healthy, transparent, loving relationship with him, we will always feel a sense of deficiency. Something will always be missing. We will never find the lasting happiness and wholeness we seek. Ultimately, only God can fill our emptiness, supply our lack, and satisfy our needs.

When Jesus Works a Room

When Jesus was physically here on earth, what would it have been like to be Mary or Martha or Lazarus or one of the disciples? What would it have been like to shoot the breeze with Jesus? To have a barbecue with Jesus? What would the conversations have been about?

I think they would have been all about adding value to you. About listening to you. About serving you. About loving you. When Jesus was in any sort of social context, do you know what his natural reaction was? To serve. When he met someone, his first thought was, *How can I serve this person?* He came into social settings thinking, *How can I encourage other people here?*

Why? Because he was full. He didn't need anything from anyone. He came simply to add, to serve, to complete. His idea of "working a room" was not networking and smooth-talking and manipulating people for his own benefit. It was to make sure everyone walked out feeling better, thinking better, and knowing God better than when they walked in.

Jesus is the guy you want as your friend. He wants to give to you, not take from you. He enjoys being with you because of who you are, not because of what you can do for him. Jesus is not consumed with himself.

You've probably met a few people who are truly secure.

They have a sense of contentment in their lives. They know who they are. They are not concerned with comparison or competition, but they are at rest and at peace, and they continually add value to others. Maybe you are one of those people. I know I want to be one.

I want to live like Jesus. I know that's a bit of a cliché sometimes, but I really mean it. Jesus always seemed to find creative ways to add value to people. You know that kind of person—no matter how bad the meal was you just cooked, they find a way to compliment it. No matter how crazy your kids are behaving, they find a way to make you feel like amazing parents of amazing children.

Can you imagine what it would look like if all of us—families, friends, churches—lived and related and loved from a place of inner fullness? I think it would look a lot like heaven on earth.

Bad News, Good News

John said, "We have received from his fullness" (John 1:16, paraphrased). How do we receive? We don't earn it. We don't deserve it. We don't develop it. We simply trust it, believe it, and receive it. Our mind-set should be, *God, I receive from you fullness today. I am who I am by your grace. I find my rest and contentment and peace in who you are through me.*

I'm not talking about repeating some formula or magic prayer, of course. I'm talking about becoming aware of what

God has already made available to us. We can receive from Jesus' fullness to the point where we are emotionally, mentally, and spiritually complete and full.

This eradicates one of the greatest hurdles in relationships, friendships, and community: insecurity.

Insecurity is more than just an emotion: it is a deep sense of incompleteness, imperfection, deficiency, and lack. It paralyzes us relationally and socially, and it isolates us. People can be all around us, yet we feel profoundly alone because we think we don't measure up or we aren't good enough.

I've got bad news and good news. The bad news is, we are right in our self-assessment. We don't measure up and we aren't good enough. But the good news is, Jesus is enough. He's more than enough, actually, and if we lean on him and receive from him, we will be enough as well.

Sometimes we think our personality types define our social skills, but that is not true. We all need friends. We all need community. When we find our security and completeness in Jesus, his fullness transcends our personality types and helps us become better friends, better spouses, better parents, better employees, and better neighbors.

It's amazing how many people I run into in their forties, fifties, and sixties who say, "I just don't have any good friends anymore." You would think it would be easier to make friends the older we get, but in fact, it's often harder. We get burned, we get disillusioned, we get manipulated, and eventually we give up. We start to keep people at arm's length to protect ourselves.

Jesus wants to heal the hurts and remove the scar tissue. He wants to help us relate socially the way he did—thinking of others and serving others. Ironically, we are most protected against hurt not when we withdraw and isolate ourselves, but when we serve others with no strings attached.

Jesus is the relationship that completes us. When we find true friendship in him, it frees us to discover real relationship with fellow human beings on this planet at a level we never thought possible.

Jesus is the one who fills us. And when we're full, we're free.

Conclusion

I don't think any human has figured out life completely. We're on a journey of self-discovery and God-discovery. My goal in this book has not been to tell you how to live, but rather to point you to the source and the focus of life itself: Jesus. When we see Jesus for who he is, when we begin to learn from him and follow him, we discover satisfaction, joy, and peace that we never imagined.

I hope this book has been a catalyst for your own journey with God. He loves you and he believes in you. He knows you better than you know yourself. He sees your good moments and your not-so-good moments, and no matter what you might think of yourself, he is unequivocally proud of you and passionately in love with you.

I encourage you to take time to learn about God and to learn from God. He desires the best for you, and following his principles and priorities will only make your life better.

Remember, God is what makes the four statements at the heart of this book work:

1. Life is to be loved and to love.
2. Life is to trust God in every moment.
3. Life is to be at peace with God and yourself.
4. Life is to enjoy God.

The ball is in your court now. Ahead of you is the rest of your life. And know this: you can't fail. No matter what, God will love you and draw you to himself. He is with you and he is for you.

Life is waiting for you, and it is amazing.

Acknowledgments

Jesus,
Chelsea,
Zion,
Eliott,
Grace,
Dad,
Mom,
Family,
Friends,
The City Church,
Thomas Nelson,
Esther,
Justin,
Aunt Barb,
Leon,
B.J.,
and thank you, Carla, for being a constant
source of wisdom, strength, and sanity.

About the Author

Judah and Chelsea Smith are the lead pastors of the City Church based in Seattle, Washington. Judah is a well-known speaker at conferences and churches around the world. His humorous yet poignant messages demystify the Bible and show people who Jesus is in their everyday lives. Judah is the author of the *New York Times* bestseller *Jesus Is* ____.

Before assuming the lead pastorate in 2009, Judah led the youth ministry of the City Church for ten years. He has authored several books and is a popular voice on Twitter (@judahsmith).

Judah and Chelsea have three children: Zion, Eliott, and Grace. Judah is an avid golfer and all-around sports fan. He believes the Seahawks are God's favorite team and is praying for the Sonics to come back to Seattle.

LIFE IS _____. How Would You Finish that Sentence?

Judah Smith believes Jesus shows us how to live life to the fullest. In this six-session video study, Judah completes the new sentence again and again, revealing how

- **LIFE IS** _to be loved and to love_.
- **LIFE IS** _to trust God in every moment_.
- **LIFE IS** _to be at peace with God and yourself_.
- **LIFE IS** _to enjoy God_.

Judah speaks as a friend, welcoming new believers, lifelong followers of Jesus, and even the merely curious. He shows us the love of God that defies human logic and the life that God intends for us to have in the here and now. With excitement and humor, Judah looks at the stories in the Bible from his unique angle and shows how life is all about loving God and loving others.

For more information visit LifeIsBook.tv